Vocational Training and Placement of the Severely Handicapped

VOCATIONAL OPPORTUNITIES

Paul F. Cook
Peter R. Dahl
Margaret Ann Gale

The American Institutes for Research
in the Behavioral Sciences

OLYMPUS PUBLISHING COMPANY

Salt Lake City

1978

This work was developed under a contract with the U.S. Office of Education, Department of Health, Education, and Welfare. However, the content does not necessarily reflect the position or policy of that Agency, and no official endorsement of these materials should be inferred.

Library of Congress Cataloging in Publication Data

Cook, Paul F.   1936-
    Vocational opportunities.

    At head of title: Vocational Training and Placement
of the Severely Handicapped.
    Bibliography: p.
    Includes index.
    1. Physically handicapped--Employment--United States.
2. Vocational rehabilitation--United States.
I. Dahl, Peter R., 1946-   joint author. II. Gale,
Margaret Ann, 1943-   joint author. III. Vocational
Training and Placement of the Severely Handicapped
(Project). IV. Title.
HV3018.C66   331.5'9   78-19163
ISBN 0-913420-79-4

ACKNOWLEDGMENTS

The Vocational Training and Placement of the Severely Handicapped project was a comprehensive assessment effort involving the contributions of a large number of people, both AIR staff and a National Advisory Panel. The wide variety of contributions makes it difficult to accurately credit ideas, techniques, and suggestions to their originators.

The members of the National Advisory Panel were most helpful in their advice, suggestions, and criticisms.

National Advisory Panel

Everett Barton
Ralph Bohn
Gordon Christian
M. Harry Jennison, M.D.
Merle Karnes
Russell Kirbey
Herbert Kramer

Charles Richman
Norman Silberberg
David Taxis
Elsie Vickery
Ernest Willenberg
Tom Williamson
William E. Johnston, Jr.,
    Ex-Officio Member

Internal AIR Advisors

Albert Chalupsky   Robert Weisgerber

Project Staff

John E. Bowers and James A. Dunn, Principal Investigators
Paul F. Cook and B. Gordon Funk, Project Directors

Sibyl Anderson
Judith A. Appleby
John J. Appleby
Melanie Austin
D. Carol Bain
Nancy A. Christensen
Peter R. Dahl
Barbara Dodson

Phyllis A. Dubois
Margaret A. Gale
Susan Hanson
Carol B. Kaplan
Deborah Plumley
Jane Spangler
Debra Thomason
Irene Yurash

Preface

THE NEED   The national conscience is becoming more sensitive to the fact that many segments of American society do not receive the benefits to which they are entitled. This heightened sensitivity has led to expanded efforts to help the handicapped participate in the social, economic, and cultural mainstream of this society.

Legislation and court decisions are slowly providing the handicapped with their full civil rights as guaranteed by the Constitution, including full access to education and vocational training. However, as these legal steps are taken, the public must acknowledge the need of all handicapped people to be treated as full-fledged human beings--no longer to be unnecessarily institutionalized, regarded as second-class citizens, or denied the full benefits of American life.

In the last decade, much progress has been made in preparing the handicapped for gainful employment. Two significant steps taken during this time were the specific funding of vocational training for the handicapped in the Vocational Education Amendments of 1968 and 1976. Supported by this legislation, a number of innovative and high-quality programs for the handicapped are now operating in local school districts and other agencies.

Another significant step in improving legislation was the passage in 1975 of the Education for All Handicapped Children Act (Public Law 94-142). This bill calls for massive expansion in authorized levels of the basic state grants program. The act has three major aspects: (1) it has no expiration date; (2) it makes a specific commitment to _all_ handicapped children; and (3) it states that education must be extended to handicapped children as their fundamental right. The following are more specific implications of this legislation.

- Individualized educational programming is an essential component of appropriate education designed to meet the unique needs of handicapped children.

- To the maximum extent appropriate, handicapped children should receive education with children who are not handicapped; in other words, special classes, separate schooling, or any other removal of the handicapped from the regular educational environment should be reduced as much as possible.

- Adequate testing should be provided to ensure that student placement is not racially or culturally discriminatory. Testing will be conducted in the child's native language or mode of communication unless it is clearly not feasible to do so.

Adherence to the requirements of these implications will help eliminate the barriers currently facing severely handicapped persons as they try to find employment.

While progress is being made in helping those classified as handicapped to maximize their potential for self-fulfillment and for useful and meaningful participation in society, much more needs to be done to help the severely handicapped. "Severely handicapped" persons are those who because of the severity of their problems need educational, social, psychological, and medical services beyond those offered by traditional and special education programs. Severely handicapped persons are seriously emotionally disturbed, profoundly or severely mentally retarded, or multiply handicapped. Also in this category are persons with severe language deprivations, perceptual-cognitive deprivations, a fragile physiological condition, and/or a number of abnormal behaviors. Abnormal behaviors may include a failure to attend to pronounced social stimuli, self-mutilation, durable and intense temper tantrums, and the absence of rudimentary verbal control. The impairment of the severely handicapped is considered to be relatively permanent (U.S. Office of Education, Bureau of Education for the Handicapped, 1975).

THE PROJECT   The Bureau of Education for the Handicapped (BEH) of the U.S. Office of Education has outlined two principal objectives for improving the fortunes of the severely handicapped: first, ". . . to enable the most severely handicapped children and youth to become as independent as possible, thereby reducing their requirement for institutional care and providing opportunity for self-development;" second, ". . . to stimulate the initiation, expansion, and improvement of vocational education programs for the handicapped throughout the country in order to assure that every handicapped youth will have career education training which is relevant to the job market, meaningful to his career aspirations, and realistic to his fullest potential."

In July 1975 BEH contracted with the American Institutes for Research to investigate and assess the vocational training and employment possibilities of persons with severe permanent handicaps. The AIR project is called Vocational Training and Placement of the Severely Handicapped (VOTAP), and its purpose is to provide information that will help to increase the vocational education and employment opportunities for such individuals.

A National Advisory Panel was formed to provide policy orientation and technical direction to the project, and to obtain expert assistance concerning the general objectives of the project, the clientele it addresses, current and prospective training and placement methodologies, and products. The panelists were drawn from the vocational education, special education, and rehabilitation communities. The last section of this preface consists of a list of panel members.

Early in the project it became desirable to clarify that the focus of the VOTAP project was to be on vocational or occupational education rather than career education even though the BEH objective cited above implied that career education aspects should be considered. Vocational education and training in VOTAP was conceived of as education or training related to the occupational development of the severely handicapped, age 14 and beyond. This definition went beyond "vocational education" in the narrow sense of the term, which implies skills training with a trade orientation.

Although the programs to be studied by VOTAP were for students 14 years and up, it was apparent that severely handicapped persons are especially in need of occupational preparation before age 14, when prevocational training usually begins. For this reason, it was decided to include recommendations that may extend research and development activities down into the grade school and preschool years, but no attempt was made to deal with career education concerns in a comprehensive manner.

The specific objectives of the VOTAP project were to determine the following:

- What are the potential vocations for severely handicapped youth and adults?

- What vocational training programs are available for the severely handicapped?

- Do effective job placement programs exist? If so, where, and what services do they provide?

- What research and development activities might contribute to improved career/vocational education opportunities for the severely handicapped?

Project activities were to be conducted throughout with an eye to the dissemination and use of the resulting products. Appropriate education professionals were to be kept aware of the project and their assistance solicited as needed. The products resulting from the project were to be packaged in a form that facilitated their use.

The VOTAP project included five major activities. The first task was the preparation of an annotated bibliography of materials concerned with job placement of the severely handicapped.

The second task was to survey training and placement programs, to obtain descriptive data about them, and to identify particularly innovative or effective practices. Programs were selected from nominations according to geographic location, size, type of institution (public or private), and handicapping conditions of the clientele. Of the 333 programs surveyed, 169 programs responded. Guidelines for recognizing effective, innovative practices were drafted by the VOTAP project staff and were then reviewed by VOTAP's 13-member National Advisory Panel.

The third task was to prepare a handbook entitled <u>Vocational Opportunities</u>. This handbook identifies and discusses major barriers preventing the severely handicapped from obtaining vocational training and employment, and includes a description of strategies that can be used to surmount these barriers. The handbook contains lists of jobs obtained from the VOTAP survey that severely handicapped workers presently hold in sheltered workshops and competitive employment; it also contains suggestions as to how potential jobs may be opened to handicapped persons by managing relevant barriers.

The fourth task was to prepare a second handbook entitled <u>Training Programs and Placement Services</u>. This handbook contains one- to three-page descriptions of 152 programs. Innovative or effective practices are highlighted.

These practices were identified from survey returns and reviewed by using criteria drafted by the AIR research staff and critiqued by VOTAP's National Advisory Panel and by BEH.

The last major task was to prepare a monograph entitled Research and Development Recommendations. This monograph synthesizes the project findings and offers recommendations for further research and development in the area of vocational training and placement of the severely handicapped. These recommendations are based on needs identified during the course of the project and on suggestions made by the National Advisory Panel.

NATIONAL ADVISORY PANEL

Dr. Everett Barton
Facilities Specialist
California Department of Rehabilitation
Sacramento, California

Dr. Ralph Bohn
Dean of Continuing Education
San Jose State University
San Jose, California

Mr. Gordon Christian
OJT Coordinator
National Association for Retarded Citizens
Burlingame, California

M. Harry Jennison, M.D.
Executive and Medical Director
Children's Hospital at Stanford
Palo Alto, California

Dr. Merle Karnes
Director, Colonel Wolfe School
Professor of Special Education
Institute for Research in Exceptional Children
University of Illinois at Urbana-Champaign

Mr. Russell Kirbey
Executive Director
Braille Institute of America
Los Angeles, California

Dr. Herbert J. Kramer
Director of Communications
Joseph P. Kennedy, Jr. Foundation
Hartford, Connecticut

Mr. Charles Richman
Director of Product Development
International Association of Rehabilitation Facilities
Washington, D.C.

Contents

Using This Handbook

PURPOSE   This handbook describes major barriers confronted by the severely handicapped person who attempts to obtain vocational training and eventual job placement. It also describes strategies for surmounting these barriers. These strategies may be used by the individual worker, by training and placement institutions, or by other advocates seeking to help the handicapped person attain his or her occupational goals.

This handbook identifies potential jobs and vocational areas for severely handicapped persons. First, it identifies jobs at which persons with severe handicaps have been successful. Then, using the Dictionary of Occupational Titles (DOT) system of classification, the handbook shows how potential jobs can be extrapolated by identifying jobs that have similar worker requirements. Suggestions are made for opening the way to new jobs by managing the barriers that handicapped workers face in obtaining and performing these jobs. The job and skill listings are not exhaustive; they are, however, representative of the achievements of handicapped persons.

This handbook is intended primarily for use by those who provide vocational training and job placement services for the severely handicapped or by those who train personnel who will be providing these services. The handbook will be useful in:

- identifying jobs that are suitable for sheltered workshops or for competitive employment situations;

- designing programs to train people in skills relevant to a wide range of jobs or to train them in background skills that will transfer to a range of more specific training programs;

- identifying job clusters that may be open for development to persons with certain types of handicaps; and

- providing information to handicapped persons themselves, to their parents, to personnel attempting "mainstreaming" of the handicapped into the public schools, and to employers.

Following are two illustrations of how information in this handbook could be used in providing services for the severely handicapped.

Placement programs may be developed by using the information in this handbook. Setting up such a program involves two steps. First, potential jobs and employers in a community must be located. The objective of this step is to assess the local employment situation so that the training process can be realistically directed toward employment opportunities. Information on the job areas represented in the community should be systematically collected and catalogued in a central file according to appropriate characteristics, for example, work area or field, type of industry, size of institution, name of contact, extent to which each requires skills that persons with various handicaps can acquire (Peterson & Jones, 1976). The central file should be cross-

referenced to other forms and to clients, and should be updated as required--
as businesses change, as employers experience success with handicapped persons,
or as changes occur in the training and placement program. The second step is
to review job opportunities with specific employers. Contacts should be made
with employers identified in completing the first step. While individual contacts are desirable, and in some cases most effective, group contacts may
cover more ground and in the long run be as effective. A group contact would
include meetings with groups of employers or their representatives. Later,
individual employers can be contacted for discussion of specific job prospects
(Peterson & Jones, 1976).

The lists of jobs and potential jobs identified in this handbook will be useful in assessing the local employment situation. Employers can be sought out
who employ people at these or similar jobs, and training programs can be developed around these jobs or job clusters. Additionally, the handbook can be
used to provide evidence to a potential employer that handicapped persons have
succeeded in jobs similar to those in their businesses. This kind of information should be important in convincing potential employers that they may con-
fidently hire handicapped persons.

Job redesign for the handicapped (Peterson & Jones, 1976) is another area in
which information from the handbook may be useful. The purpose of job redesign is to alter jobs so that they can be done by the handicapped. It is
expected that this strategy would be used with employers who have indicated a
willingness to hire handicapped individuals but who feel that they do not have
suitable jobs available for them. The procedure outlined below is an example
of how reorganization of an employer's present job categories would permit the
placement of a handicapped person.

1. Survey of the Employer's Job Situation. By observation and discussion
    with the employer or his or her representatives, obtain information about
    job possibilities for the handicapped person who is under consideration.
    Job areas identified in this handbook are potentially fruitful leads.
    Many of them may be the same or parallel to those listed in the Worker
    Trait Group tables of this handbook and, therefore, may be obvious possi-
    bilities for employment. Other jobs may need to be analyzed in order to
    identify the job activity requirements found within them (Peterson &
    Jones, 1976).

2. Analyzing a Group of Jobs. Once the general job situation is known, study
    a few of the jobs more intensively. Solicit the employer's help in chang-
    ing jobs that have a functional or physical relationship to each other and
    that present minimal problems in reorganizing the activities and require-
    ments. The jobs should also be in high demand and offer frequent openings.

    Within the job group, identify the specific activity requirements, again
    by observation and discussion. For those that are inappropriate for a
    handicapped person, new requirements should be developed. List the activ-
    ities found in the job group, indicating the percentage of time spent in
    each activity. Also provide estimates of the personal characteristics
    required by each revised job.

3. <u>Redesigning the Job Requirements</u>. Without changing the number of jobs, regroup the activities and requirements of the selected jobs and sort them into a series of new jobs in which activities and requirements are as much alike as possible. To illustrate, if the activities and requirements of five jobs are arranged in order of difficulty and five new jobs are designed on the basis of this listing, a mentally retarded person may be able to do the job whose activities are at the bottom of the list. If this is the case, the retarded person will be performing unskilled functions formerly done by a semiskilled worker. The employer benefits from this redesign of the job because the more skilled worker is freed from doing the unskilled or less skilled work. At the same time it opens a job for a handicapped worker who can perform the unskilled tasks in a perfectly acceptable manner (Peterson & Jones, 1976). The manner in which activities and requirements are redesigned will depend upon the handicap of the individual worker. If the worker is orthopedically handicapped, job activities will be ordered by the physical requirements of mobility or lifting. If the worker is emotionally handicapped, job redesign may proceed according to the level of personal interaction, the variety of tasks to be performed, or some other relevant criterion.

SOME CAUTIONS IN THE USE OF THIS HANDBOOK

It is important to note two cautions in using this handbook.

- Information contained here cannot substitute for a careful, individual assessment of the capabilities, needs, and wants of the individual. Generalizations about handicapping conditions are useful for conceptualizing and conveying information, but they must be used cautiously when dealing with individuals. In considering the handicapped person, the needs, capabilities, and traits of the individual are paramount, not the handicapping category or condition.

- This handbook is not intended to reflect actual training or job possibilities in business and industry in every geographical area. Obviously, the job market will vary from area to area. Indeed, one of the first steps in training and placing a handicapped person is to identify those jobs in the community for which he or she might be successfully trained.

job clusters

CLUSTERING SCHEME AND
RATIONALE

Considerable attention was given to the selection of a suitable occupational clustering scheme for this handbook. The vocational training field is replete with schemes that generally include economic, individual competencies, individual interests, and manpower training models.

Occupations in the economic model are clustered around economic centers in our society. The scheme of fifteen career clusters developed by the U.S. Office of Education is an example of an economic model. Its essential purpose is to predict groupings that are likely to occur in the future labor market in the United States. Clustering is based on similarity of broad economic activities in which enterprises are engaged, for example, business and office, marketing and distribution, and communication and media.

In the individual competencies models, consideration is also given to abilities, interests, and aptitudes. This scheme is based on the assumption that a large number of jobs are open for which an individual can qualify, and the cluster forms the basis for individual guidance. Examples of individual competencies models are the Project TALENT clusters developed by Flanagan and associates (Flanagan et al., 1973), and the third edition of the Dictionary of Occupational Titles (DOT; U.S. Department of Labor, 1965). The fourth edition, which this handbook is based on, uses the individual interests model.

The manpower training models were developed primarily for technical training in industry. Clusters in this model are based on task and skill commonalities. All jobs requiring similar skills are grouped to form a cluster, and training programs are developed to emphasize skills common to many occupations. An illustration is the Maryland Cluster Design used in vocational training (Maley, 1975), which groups occupations into construction, metal forming and fabrication, and electronic-mechanical installations and repair.

The DOT is organized into nine categories:

> Professional, Technical, and Managerial
>
> Clerical and Sales
>
> Service
>
> Agricultural, Fishery, Forestry, and related occupations
>
> Processing
>
> Machine-Trades
>
> Benchwork
>
> Structural Work
>
> Miscellaneous

Each category is divided into groups of related occupations. For example, Service Occupations include:

1. Domestic Service
2. Barbering, Cosmetology, and related occupations
3. Apparel and Furnishing Services
4. Protective Services

For further information on the DOT clustering scheme, see the Appendix, p. 151.

barriers to training and employment

A CONCEPTUAL FRAMEWORK	What is a handicap? From an employer's viewpoint, a handicap is a deficit in the resources, relative to the demands of a job, that a person brings to that job (Baroff, 1973). For example, a person who cannot see well is handicapped in a job that requires good vision; if a job requires mobility, an immobile person is handicapped; or, if a job requires carefully reasoned decisions, a person unable to think things through is handicapped.

From an individual's viewpoint, a handicap is a condition that interferes with obtaining a desirable job. The condition may make it difficult to train for a job that the person could perform successfully if he or she were trained, for example, a blind person who wishes to learn auto mechanics. Similarly, a handicapping condition may make it difficult to secure a job that the person could successfully perform, for example, a paraplegic who has difficulty getting to and from work. Finally, such a condition may directly affect the person's ability to perform on the job, for example, a deaf or speech-impaired person who wishes to teach.

Thus, in considering handicaps in relation to work, one must go beyond the handicapping condition(s) and ask about the practical importance of the particular condition relative to job training, job placement, and job success. One useful approach, and the one adopted here, is to consider handicaps as conditions that cause the person to confront barriers to achievement in excess of those confronted by the nonhandicapped, and to identify strategies for overcoming these barriers so that successful training and placement can be achieved.

THERE ARE MANY TYPES OF BARRIERS

Barriers may exist within a person (internal) or an environment (external). Most situations involve a combination of barriers, but for the present purposes, discussing them separately will be useful. To illustrate, some internal barriers are the inability to see, to hear, to communicate, to think; other internal barriers include a lack of physical coordination, lack of motivation, inability to attend to one's surroundings, or a lack of perseverance at tasks. External barriers, on the other hand, related to the physical environment and to the behavior and attitudes of others in that environment toward the severely handicapped. Examples of external barriers are a lack of transportation and unreachable or unusable public facilities such as telephones, drinking fountains, counters, and sidewalks. Some other external barriers are bias, prejudice, indifference, and lack of social acceptance, parental support, or understanding by others.

In regard to jobs, a handicapping condition may be a barrier to at least three facets of the job. First, the condition may be a barrier to actual task performance, as in the case of the deaf-mute who wishes to teach. The second facet is job selection; a handicapping condition may be a barrier to training or placement, although the condition may have nothing to do with the ability to perform. The blind auto mechanic illustrates such difficulties, as do the problems often faced by epileptics who find the doors closed to many jobs even through their seizures are controlled. The third facet is job retention, and a handicapping condition may be a barrier to this goal. A handicapped person with an extreme cosmetic condition, for example, may alienate fellow workers and, regardless of his or her ability to do the work, may lose the job.

BARRIERS VARY IN IMPORTANCE	In a sense, of course, all people are handicapped in that everyone has at least some resource deficits relative to the demands of certain jobs. For example, it is difficult for a short person to be a professional basketball player or for an exceptionally tall person to fit into the cockpit of a fighter plane; not everyone has the finger dexterity to be a professional pianist, and many persons cannot think with the logic and precision necessary to be a computer programmer. Thus, one must consider the importance of a handicapping condition in terms of the extent to which the individual's condition makes it difficult to train for, be placed in, or to succeed at a desirable job. All the severely handicapping conditions of concern in this handbook lead to many major barriers for those who have such conditions.
	Another point to clarify is that handicapping conditions are not all equally relevant to task performance, job selection, or job retention. Strategies for training and job placement should be chosen for the handicapped person based on the relevance of the handicapping condition. For example, placing a handicapped person in a job in which the handicapping condition is irrelevant to the job should not be difficult if the person possesses the nonhandicapped-related resources. On the other hand, if the handicapping condition is relevant, it may be an impediment rather than an insurmountable barrier. Barriers do not represent all-or-nothing conditions. Visual deficits, for example, are not insurmountable; jobs in which sight is important may be modified so that tasks requiring sight are minimized. The mentally retarded overcome many barriers and perform tasks of surprising complexity given effective training techniques and time (Gold, 1972, 1973, 1974; Gold & Barclay, 1973).
DESCRIPTION OF BARRIER TABLES	The tables that follow identify types of barriers that handicapped workers face in their attempts to gain relevant vocational training and job placement. Attitudes, skills, communication, and environment are the major barrier groups. Within each of these major barrier groups, functional barriers are listed and some strategies for overcoming them are provided. Examples of how these strategies may be applied are also given.

12

barrier tables

Barrier 1.0   Attitudes

Handicapped persons, or those with whom they deal, frequently hold
unrealistic attitudes regarding the individual worth, potential, or
competence of handicapped persons. For the handicapped themselves,
this may give rise to inappropriate feelings of unworthiness, help-
lessness, or inferiority. Examples of attitudes manifested by the
nonhandicapped are failure to appreciate the contributions that
handicapped workers can make, discomfort when associating with obviously handicapped people, and fear of increased insurance rates
or of a detrimental effect on the company image.

Attitudes may be regarded as underlying learned predispositions that
exert a consistent influence on an individual's evaluative responses.
In trying to produce changes in the self-concepts of handicapped
persons, getting them to say they think more highly of themselves is
not sufficient; rather, the goal is to have the handicapped behave
in a variety of changed ways--toward themselves, toward other handicapped people, and toward the nonhandicapped. Psychologists generally divide attitudes into three components: affective, cognitive,
and behavioral. Techniques designed to change only a person's emotional reactions toward another person attack only one component of
the attitude in question. This point partially explains why attitude
modification is a difficult and sometimes unsuccessful process.
Simply giving people information is not enough. Research has indicated that active participation, as in roleplaying, is more effective
in changing attitudes than is passive exposure to persuasive communications (Zimbardo & Ebbesen, 1969).

Functional Barrier 1.1 LACK OF KNOWLEDGE REGARDING CONSEQUENCES OF HIRING THE DISABLED

Employers mistakenly believe that if they hire the severely disabled their insurance rates will increase, they will have increased costs for training and adapting their working environment, and customers and other employees will react adversely to associating with obviously handicapped people.

STRATEGIES FOR OVERCOMING THIS BARRIER

EDUCATION

Employers should be educated so that they know that workmen's compensation insurance rates do not increase when the handicapped are employed. Insurance rates are determined by the type of work conducted, not by the characteristics of the employees. Insurance companies should continue to inform policy holders that hiring the severely disabled is encouraged and will not adversely affect a company's insurance rates (American Mutual Insurance Alliance).

Another component of employer education should focus on the potential positive aspect of having handicapped persons function successfully with nonhandicapped workers. In some cases morale of nonhandicapped employees has improved, as exemplified by fewer employee complaints and reduced criticism about their jobs.

In order to make employers and co-workers comfortable in the process of interviewing and working with the severely disabled, seminars, filmstrips, and printed matter that explain how to react to the severely disabled should be provided. Such training aids could be provided by nonprofit organizations, federal and state agencies, and professional business associations and should include practical, everyday advice such as the following, suggested by the President's Committee on Employment of the Handicapped:

1. Stop thinking of impaired people as "disabled." This description was adopted to soften the word "crippled," but the connotations of "disabled" are even more painful. The word implies across-the-board inability to perform, and this is not true.

2. Don't dismiss the idea of employing impaired workers without finding out what they can do on a fair and equitable basis.

3. Let these workers compete. Many people, in a sincere effort to help, actually make things more difficult for the handicapped. **The human and economic needs of the handicapped are best served when they are allowed to become self-supporting and, thereby, to make their contributions as self-reliant members of society.**

4. Recognize the handicapped as individuals and deal with them accordingly. Sometimes their physical problems limit the scope of their activities, but they should be considered and recognized for their individual skills.

5. Don't patronize people with physical disabilities. The handicapped don't want to be coddled or fussed over.

LEGISLATIVE ACTION

Legislative action regarding the employment of the handicapped is one method of overcoming attitude barriers. For example. Section 503 of the Rehabilitation Act of 1973 contains a strong affirmative action clause for organizations utilizing federal monies after January 1976. Every federal agency contract of more than $2,500 requires that qualified handicapped applicants be actively recruited, considered, and employed, and that all qualified handicapped employees be afforded nondiscriminatory consideration for promotion and job advancement. No handicapped individual may be discriminated against on the basis of a handicap. Additional legislation will be required to define discrimination and to determine when an abuse occurs. And since business/industry is often hesitant to hire the handicapped, the handicapped need to acquire a social militance to pressure employers to consider them for employment (U.S. Department of Labor, Manpower Administration).

RESPONSIBILITIES OF EMPLOYERS

Employers should be encouraged to seek the cooperation of management, employees, and union personnel in a campaign to develop affirmative action plans and to hire qualified handicapped employees. As part of this effort, employers should:

1. Actively recruit persons with disabilities.

2. Analyze their hiring processes by reevaluating the emphasis given to medical histories in the screening process. Physical examinations should be used for selective <u>placement</u> and not for selective <u>elimination</u>. Employers might consider giving examinations in nontraditional ways.

3. Restructure or modify jobs to reduce the effect of a disability on a worker's performance. This may require making hours more flexible; splitting one job between a handicapped person and another part-time employee; and designing a "sheltered enclave" for handicapped workers.

4. Change equipment or add adaptive devices to make the job situation more amenable to the needs of handicapped persons. In some circumstances, the employer's State Department of Rehabilitation may provide handicapped persons with specialized equipment that will help them do their jobs.

5. Adopt the 700-hour temporary trial appointment system, used by the Civil Service Commission, for severely handicapped persons.

6. Offer consultation services to rehabilitation workshops and to local school districts and volunteer to serve on local vocational education advisory committees.

Functional Barrier 1.2   LOW EXPECTANCY ON THE PART OF SOCIETY

People working with the handicapped decide, on the basis of their own experiences, the performance capabilities of the handicapped. They then, as a self-fulfilling prophecy, seek to prove themselves to be right. As a result, the handicapped people they work with do only what is expected of them. Severely handicapped workers are conceived of as permanent members of a surplus labor force; hence, no really rewarding job situations are developed for them.

STRATEGIES FOR OVERCOMING THIS BARRIER

DEVELOPMENT OF GENUINE COMPETENCIES

Emerging technologies designed to help individuals who find learning difficult may be utilized. Examples of these technologies include discrimination learning, attention-retention theory, behavior modification, and such specific techniques as matching-to-sample, oddity, clustering, fading, and shaping (Gold, 1975). The goal is to produce skill on the job when removal from the job would require training another worker. To illustrate, a 21-year-old severely retarded male was taught to complete the assembly of 52-piece cam switch actuator. Training was accomplished by dividing the task into 52 steps, each of which involved both manipulation and discrimination components. The use of bins, a metal stabilizing post, two types of retaining ring tools, and tweezers was required. In a six-month period the handicapped worker's production rate ranged from 74% to 133% of normal; his monthly earnings (piece rate) ranged from $76.86 to $131.46, with a monthly average of $99.69 and an hourly average of $1.00 (Bellamy, Peterson, & Close, 1975).

PUBLIC AWARENESS

Obtain media coverage to make the public aware of the successes of handicapped workers in a variety of jobs.

Functional Barrier 1.3   LOW SELF-ESTEEM

> This barrier involves a set of personal attitudes that behaviorally manifests itself in a lack of interest in job training or possibilities, withdrawal from learning and working situations, a lack of persistence in difficult tasks, ready discouragement, lack of personal planning, etc.

STRATEGIES FOR OVERCOMING THIS BARRIER

SUPPORTIVE COUNSELING

Counseling may be accomplished either individually or in groups, while in training or after a person has been placed on the job. It may be done by a single counselor or by a team. The intent is to foster self-reliance and to encourage clients to undertake appropriate work tasks. For example, the Sacramento Society for the Blind established an intensive five-week vocational course for young adults 15 to 20 years old. The Self-Reliance Institute operated on three basic assumptions: first, that blind adolescents behave according to the expectations of those around them; second, that they are essentially underachievers with poor self-images; and third, that they have a latent capacity to become productive workers. The individualized approach often used with the handicapped was abandoned in favor of a "bootcamp" attitude which pushed the group to achieve. The five-week course included part-time work experience, daily living instruction, and job placement (Laurence, 1973).

WORK EXPERIENCE

Realistic work-setting experience may be provided to the client either in a workshop setting or in a work station in industry. Supervision may be provided either by rehabilitation personnel or by the employing business or industry. Guided success in an actual work experience appears to be highly motivating. For example, the Occupational Training Center (OTC) in St. Paul, Minnesota, trained handicapped and multiply handicapped youths and adults for useful employment. New clients were evaluated by counselors and instructors on the basis of their performance during a three-week "testing-by-doing" period. If OTC could help a client, she/he was accepted and an occupational development plan was designed for her/him. OTC used task analysis and job reengineering to facilitate training and placement of the handicapped. OTC entered into agreements with several private industries in order to place their clients in actual job situations for further training. In order to prepare employees more fully for outside employment, OTC offered individual instruction units on grooming, community relations, employer expectations, and personal and social attitudes (Durand, Nelson, & O'Brien, 1973).

BEHAVIOR MODIFICATION

Behavior modification techniques may be used to reward appropriate assertive behavior (leading to a change in attitudes) either in training or in the work situation. The technique includes identifying appropriate target behaviors (either to be increased or to be decreased), obtaining baseline data, and systematically altering stimulus conditions and/or reinforcement contingencies while recording changes in target behavior. Behavioral modification techniques were used in a study of the effects of using money, social praise, and production charts as reinforcers to increase production in a collating task. Eighteen 12- to 20-year-old retarded and severely emotionally disturbed students in a public school were the subjects of the study. Differential increases in productivity were achieved. The study found that performance generally improves when reinforcers are provided; that prevocational programs in public schools are capable of providing other agencies with valuable vocational skills information for their clients; and that many severely handicapped persons either do not know how to use money or are not allowed extensive use of it even though it is the primary reinforcer in our society (Brown, VanDeventer, Perlmutter, Jones, & Sontag, 1972).

Barrier 2.0 Communication

Barriers addressed in this section arise from difficulties in receiving, apprehending, or relating information. Such difficulties
may result from sensory or motor disabilities or from processing
dysfunctions other than those caused by mental retardation. The
skills needed to establish interpersonal relationships in which
persons become more sensitive to, and effective in meeting, each
other's social and psychological needs are not covered in this
section; such skills are dealt with in the section on Attitudes.

Functional Barrier 2.1   IMPAIRED ABILITY TO SPEAK OR HEAR

> Many jobs presuppose that workers will be able to talk to one another or to customers and clients. Those who cannot speak, who have speech that is especially difficult to understand, or who have hearing impairments may need special aids or training if they are to perform such jobs satisfactorily.

STRATEGIES FOR OVERCOMING THIS BARRIER*

DEVICES THAT USE VISUAL DISPLAYS IN LIEU OF SPEECH

Lapboards (or matrix communicators) containing words, letters, or other symbols at which the user may point, have long been used by those whose disabilities exclude writing as well as speaking (Cohen, 1976). Typically, boards require relatively dexterous use of the hands or a headstick, and communication using them is usually slow.

Speed and ease of communication using lapboards can be significantly enhanced by devices that make fewer physical demands on the user. Joysticks or pressure-sensitive pads that can move a light beneath the translucent face of a lapboard is an example. This system has the added advantage of allowing the lapboard to be placed somewhere other than on the lap of the user. Thus, the board might be placed where it could be viewed conveniently by all parties to the communication. Strip printers can be incorporated into matrix communicators, allowing the handicapped worker to spell out an entire message that can then be read by a nonhandicapped colleague who can attend to other duties while the message is being spelled out (Tufts-New England Medical Center). Similarly, in job situations where relatively few commands or replies must be given frequently, strip printers that produce an entire message in response to a single movement of a joystick (TRACE Center) or that flash a light adjacent to a sentence or phrase show promise (Veterans Administration). Such devices all suffer either from being slow and tedious to use or from being relatively inflexible in the variety of messages that can be transmitted; they are most useful on jobs where frequent, rapid, or intricate communications are not required.

SPEECH AUGMENTATION OR GENERATION DEVICES

The electronic larynx amplifies softly-spoken speech, rendering a normal-sounding voice. It has been used successfully by post-laryngectomy patients and others with similar functional difficulties in speaking loudly enough to be heard. This device allows its user to operate normally in almost any situation where speech is needed.

For those who cannot speak at all or who cannot speak intelligibly, an adaptation of a calculator that voices answers to the blind shows promise. This device has a 64-work spoken vocabulary, and words can be chosen to meet the needs of the client. Wisely chosen, 64 words can express a large proportion of the commands or requests needed in many job situations.

---

*Many strategies for overcoming communications barriers involve electromechanical aids of one sort or another. Some specific devices are, therefore, discussed by way of illustration in this section. It should be understood that these discussions do not constitute a complete listing of available devices, nor do they constitute guarantees as to the suitability and availability of particular devices.

BASIC COMMUNICATION SKILLS FOR CO-WORKERS

Most co-workers will have had little experience with people who have serious trouble hearing. They will not know what to do to make communication easier. Simple tips to facilitate lipreading (NTID) can be taught quickly, as can a few basic signs. Co-workers can readily be taught to speak slowly and clearly, to face the deaf person directly, and to avoid pacing, standing in shadows, or standing before a bright background when speaking to the deaf; they can be encouraged to expand their signing and finger-spelling skills.

SPEECH THERAPY FOR CLIENTS

There are many techniques of speech and language therapy that can help people with hard-to-understand speech speak more clearly. To be most effective, a counselor or speech therapist may wish to assist during the transfer of skills from the training environment to the work place (Bentzen, 1973). As part of the transfer, the counselor may wish to help other employees learn to understand the client's speech; the ability of others to understand the client may improve more rapidly if the therapist serves as a "translator" or provides other help. Such assistance may smooth the way for persons with any of the large number of handicapping conditions that can make speech difficult to understand.

Functional Barrier 2.2 IMPAIRED ABILITY TO READ OR TO REVIEW ONE'S OWN WRITTEN WORK

Many jobs require a person to read or to prepare documents, memoranda, diagrams, and similar materials. Inability to do so is a serious problem for many multiply handicapped people, primarily those with visual impairments. Physical diabilities that cause difficulties in using typewriters are discussed under Functional Barrier 2.3.

STRATEGIES FOR OVERCOMING THIS BARRIER

"CONVERSION" OF PRINT TO SOUND OR TOUCH

The OPTACON (Optical to Tactile Converter) consists of a small camera and an electronics section. When the user moves the camera across a line of type, the electronics section converts the light pattern into a tactile pattern that can be felt through an opening in the electronics section (Telesensory Systems).

The Steretoner (Mauch Laboratories) is physically and conceptually similar to the OPTACON, but differs in that it converts the printed stimulus into a tone pattern. Such devices may be especially useful in technical fields where typeface variation is minimal (e.g., computer printouts) or where technical symbols and schematic drawings must be read (e.g., engineering and architecture). In the latter case, the elimination of the need for the production of raised-line drawings or laborious verbal descriptions by associates would be particularly advantageous.

A problem with these devices is that their normal use requires good fine motor coordination to "track" the camera across lines of type. For persons with relatively minor motor difficulties, a guide such as that developed for training beginning OPTACON users will probably solve the problem. This guide consists of two bars crossed at 90°. The camera is attached to one bar that is pushed from left to right to move from letter to letter, thus preventing the user from straying from line to line. This bar is attached to a gasket that rides on the second bar. Pushing or pulling on this gasket allows the user to move from line to line.

For those with more serious motor handicaps (e.g., many paraplegics and those with severe cerebral palsy), more sophisticated attachments may be needed. A joystick drive for the guide described above is a technically feasible solution.

SIMULTANEOUS PRODUCTION OF BRAILLE AND INKPRINT

"Braille verifiers" produce braille copies of documents with the production of a typed copy. Such devices are useful for blind typists who can use the tape to proof their work. Braille verifiers can also be used to produce braille copies of memos and other in-house documents to which both blind and sighted workers should have access. Some braille printers can be used with computer terminals, and some computer systems can print in braille as well as ink, using standard printout formats (Triformation Systems; Protestant Guild for the Blind).

Functional Barrier 2.3   DIFFICULTY IN USING STANDARD COMMUNICATIONS EQUIPMENT

Many disabilities make it difficult for people to use standard communications devices such as telephones and typewriters. These devices, widely exploited to provide job opportunities for the homebound when used in traditional ways, are opening many new possibilities to the homebound and non-homebound alike as components in computer systems. Thus, equipment adaptations will open a larger number of rewarding jobs to capable, physically handicapped persons.

STRATEGIES FOR OVERCOMING THIS BARRIER

TYPEWRITER MODIFICATIONS

Mouthsticks, headwands, mechanical page turners, special braces, and similar appliances have long been used as aids in typing and other clerical tasks. Most of these aids are also suitable when using computer keyboards. In a demonstration study conducted by IBM and the Woodrow Wilson Rehabilitation Center (Knorr & Hammond, 1975), only relatively minor equipment modifications were required to facilitate programmer training for severely physically disabled people. Modifications included a wire frame to hold paper upright when it emerged from the carriage, enlarged copies of portions of the programming manual posted on walls for quick reference, and an electrically activated platen reverse. For those unable to operate equipment modified in these ways, other adaptations are possible; for example, a one-finger input system for programming has been developed (President's Committee on Employment of the Handicapped, 1975), as has a device that allows single-switch operation of certain electric typewriters (Library of Congress; Bush Electric Company). For those with poorly coordinated movements, special keyboards are available that make relatively modest demands in this area (Library of Congress, 1972). Such keyboards can be positioned to allow operation by hand, arm, foot, or head.

Operation of typewriters presents few problems for the blind or visually impaired, but proofreading or editing can be difficult. Braille verifiers, discussed under Functional Barrier 2.2, are valuable aids for the blind. For the visually impaired, closed circuit television attachments can be used to present enlarged images when standard magnifiers are not adequate.

SPECIAL NEEDS TELEPHONE EQUIPMENT

Commercial telephone systems offer a wide range of off-the-shelf equipment for the deaf, the hard of hearing, the blind, those with speech impairments, and the physically handicapped (Smith, 1975). In addition, custom equipment can be developed for those whose needs are not met by what is presently available. Presently available equipment includes headset amplifiers; bone conduction receivers; extra loud or restricted frequency bells for the hard of hearing; a "code-com" attachment that converts sound into light flashes and vibrations, allowing coded signals to be transmitted; devices for the deaf that blink or cause lights to blink; and special dialers and headsets that place minimal physical demands on amputees or those with restricted use of their arms and hands.

More sophisticated telecommunications systems are available that allow telephone-mediated teletype communication. Such systems allow the deaf person to receive messages over the telephone at a rate as fast as the person sending the message can type. The obvious drawback is that both sender and receiver must possess considerable equipment; the countervailing advantage is the messages are preserved on paper. Another convenient system for telephone communication with the deaf is the Manual Communication Module (MCM), a light, battery-powered portable. The console has a receptacle that is compatible with all U.S. handsets, a 32-character readout for receiving incoming messages, and a keyboard for typing the message to be transmitted.

Barrier 3.0   Environment

Many work places and pieces of equipment make demands that are basically extraneous to the tasks being performed. Such demands, whether they arise from warning lights that the blind cannot see or high shelves that those in wheelchairs cannot reach, constitute serious barriers that have little or nothing to do with job competence; yet they hinder the handicapped worker as he or she seeks to accomplish the job. Strategies discussed in this section can be used to overcome barriers that arise because of the structure of the physical environment.

Functional Barrier 3.1 INABILITY TO USE ORDINARY MEANS OF TRANSPORTATION

Few issues are as important to disabled people as accessible transportation services. Transportation can make the difference between meaningful work and mere subsistence, between sharing the community of one's friends or being isolated. The availability of accessible transportation directly affects one's quality of life.

STRATEGIES FOR OVERCOMING THIS BARRIER

EDUCATION   Architects, designers, contractors, and developers should be taught about the mobility needs of the handicapped so that they can begin designing and building barrier-free environments. In order to satisfy even the minimum requirements, the following elements of **barrier-free design should be incorporated into all building designs as well as local, state, and federal building codes** (The Rehabilitation Institute of Chicago):

1. At least one primary entrance is wheelchair accessible.
2. There are elevators between all floors.
3. All essential areas not served by elevators are accessible by an appropriately constructed ramp.
4. Places of public assembly have clear viewing spaces where persons may remain in their wheelchairs.

DESIGN   Public transportation should be designed so that vehicles are accessible to the handicapped; or specially designed buses could be provided on a case-by-case basis. As a guide to the design of public buses for the handicapped, the Regional Transportation District in Denver, Colorado contracted for buses to be built with the following characteristics:

1. wheelchair lifts
2. wheelchair tiedowns
3. extendable steps
4. bench seating
5. flip armrests
6. specially coated, non-slip handrails and stanchions
7. accessible signal tap switches
8. audible tones for doors
9. additional lighting in stepwell and door areas
10. internal public address systems

The Regional Transportation District also identified those characteristics of bus transportation which have a minimal effect on manual operation but which have a high potential **benefit for a large** percentage of transit riders. The following characteristics were **identified**:

1. Extendable steps: Extendable steps provide a low step for increased accessibilty and safety.
2. Additional grabrails and stanchions: These provide easier entrance to and exit from the buses as well as increased safety and stability inside the bus.
3. Side destination signing: A much requested feature which aids the visually impaired

Functional Barrier 3.2 INABILITY TO FUNCTION IN A BUSINESS SETTING BECAUSE OF ARCHITECTURAL BARRIERS

A number of severely handicapped persons find that moving about, including the management of transportation vehicles, is a barrier to vocational success. There are a number of carriers, including public and private transportation, escalators, and elevators, that are difficult or impossible to use. Many of the physically disabled are unable to work and move about in the average business/industrial setting because of the placement of light switches, elevator buttons, and drinking fountains. The handicapped are also inhibited by bathroom layouts, table and desk layouts, and stairs.

STRATEGIES FOR OVERCOMING THIS BARRIER

EDUCATION   Designers, architects, builders, and community planners should be taught the design elements that are needed to make buildings and facilities accessible to the handicapped. In order to satisfy the minimum requirements, the following features that eliminate barriers to the handicapped should be included (the President's Committee on Employment of the Handicapped):

1. At least one building entrance at ground level
2. 32" wide doors that open easily
3. Level thresholds to buildings and rooms
4. Sloping ramps instead of stairs (ratio--1 to 12)
5. Convenient parking, accessible to buildings
6. Access by handicapped to elevators
7. Restrooms with wide stalls and grabbars for wheelchair users
8. Handrails on all stairways where steps cannot be eliminated
9. Non-slip floors
10. Lower fountains and public telephones for wheelchair users
11. Level walks with no curbs at crossways

DESIGN   Buildings and facilities should be designed so that they eliminate barriers to the handicapped. Several organizations and publications can provide specific references regarding the redesign of drinking facilities, bathrooms, halls, light fixtures, desks, phones, ramps, etc. Of particular interest are "custom design" companies such as Independence Engineering, Inc., and publications such as Guidelines for State and Local Vocational Rehabilitation and Employment Committees (National Association for Retarded Citizens) and the Directory of Vehicles and Related Systems Components for the Elderly and Handicapped (U.S. Department of Transportation, Urban Mass Transportation Administration).

PLANNING   Employers should establish planning committees to study barriers and their elimination so that the facilities can be improved. The committees should write letters to handicapped persons inviting them to accept membership on the planning committees.

COMMUNICATION   Buildings should be clearly marked with the international symbol of access to identify accessible entrances, restrooms, and directional routes (U.S. Department of Health, Education, and Welfare).

and handicapped in bus identification.

4. Additional lighting in stepwell and door areas: A significant safety feature which aids the visually impaired during nighttime operations.
5. Spot or floodlights for outside door areas: A safety feature which aids the general public as well as the elderly and handicapped during nighttime operations.
6. Internal public address system: This is used for destination announcements, especially for the visually impaired.
7. Audio warning signal operating with door: A safety and convenience item for the audio/visually impaired.

DISSEMINATION
The specific guidelines for the design of transit buses, school buses, and other vehicles developed by the Franklin Institute Research Labs (FIRL) and published by the U.S. Department of Transportation, Urban Mass Transportation Administration, should be distributed. Distribution of the guidelines will ensure that those who design, build, or purchase such transportation equipment are aware of the requirements of the disabled. This very specific information serves as a resource of design requirements for barrier-free transportation vehicles, as well as a directory of companies and suppliers who handle special equipment and services.

COMMUNITY PARTICIPATION
Communities should consider providing vans, buses, or other vehicles designed especially for the disabled as part of ongoing rehabilitation, social, and employment services. Transportation for disabled individuals could be provided as needed or on a scheduled basis (Regional Transportation District, Denver, Colorado).

LEGISLATION
Laws regarding the removal of barriers and the provision of special accesses should be enforced. Organizations should be encouraged to conduct activities in settings that are free of architectural barriers.

Functional Barrier 3.3 DIFFICULTY IN PERCEIVING AND RESPONDING TO ENVIRONMENTAL SIGNALS

Nearly every work environment requires the worker to perceive signals, to apprehend their significance, and to behave appropriately on the basis of these signals. Signals include the obvious gauges, meters, rulers, warning lights, buzzers, and other such items. Signals, as used here, also includes environmental information that the nonhandicapped use to guide their behavior but which is inaccessible to those with certain handicaps. Visual signals arising in the natural course of work provide a ready class of examples--the proper positioning of a tool or the guiding of a board through a saw are usually done using visual information picked up from the work environment; frequently, alternate signaling systems can be found.

STRATEGIES FOR OVERCOMING THIS BARRIER

AUGMENTATION OF SYMBOLS

There are two points at which a signal may be augmented: (1) at the source of the signal by making it brighter, louder, larger, or effecting similar alteration; and (2) near the point of reception by providing the worker with an implement that will alter the signal to make it perceptible. Wherever the alteration is effected, consideration must be given to the specific needs of each individual, and to constraints that exist in the environment in which the augmentation is to take place. (For example, it would not be difficult to substitute an 8-inch gong for the usual bell on an electric typewriter to signal when the right margin is being approached; such a modification would obviously be unsatisfactory in an environment in which a hard-of-hearing typist has co-workers with normal hearing.)

In many cases, auditory or visual deficits are more severe in some frequencies or wavelengths than in others; a tone or light that capitalizes on the worker's best frequency or wavelength can be substituted for standard bells, buzzers, or lamps. If such modifications are unsatisfactory, workers can be supplied with hearing aids; magnifiers (hand held or mounted in stands or on eyeglasses); high intensity, low glare lamps; closed circuit television systems; and the like. Enlarged print can be used in manuals and diagrams for the partially sighted; enlarging lenses can be fitted to gauges and meters; or faces on gauges and meters can be enlarged or printed in colors selected to enhance readability. (For excellent discussions of aids for the visually impaired see Sloan, 1971; American Foundation for the Blind, 1976; and Sensory Aids Foundation, forthcoming.)

PRESENTATION OF SIGNALS IN A DIFFERENT MODALITY

Augmentation is not always sufficient. In such cases, a modality shift may be satisfactory. Warning lights can be replaced by bells or buzzers for those with visual handicaps, while bells and buzzers can be replaced by lights for the deaf or hard of hearing. Such systems can be made to start fans or vibrating motors if a deaf-blind person must be signaled. Such modifications are ideal warning signals for fire, equipment malfunctions, or other emergencies.

The Wrist-Com (Kruger, 1976) is particularly versatile. Attached to the wrist of the wearer, this device vibrates in response to signals transmitted to it and can be used to indicate a variety of environmental events through coded signals.

Many tools and measuring devices that have raised letters or braille letters and numerals are available for the blind (Clark, 1973). Similarly, special guides and jigs can be built to help a deaf-blind individual position tools or parts or guide materials through power equipment. Controls and other manipulative devices that are traditionally distinguished by sight can be altered to be distinguishable by touch; often this is as simple as roughing up one or two smooth knobs with a file. In other cases, more sophisticated solutions may be required, and many of these are available or are under development (Sensory Aids Foundation, forthcoming). While it is beyond the scope of this handbook to discuss all of these devices, a few will be noted: a pressure gauge for discovering leaks in refrigeration systems that buzzes when the pressure is incorrect; an audio indicator accurate to 1/1000 of an inch that allows machinists to make angular and linear measurements; and light probes that allow detection of differences in light intensity, useful in gauges and in a host of other applications (OPTACON Fund Quarterly Reports).

For performing mathematical computations, "talking" calculators that report the results of computations audibly are available for the blind, as are others that supply results in braille. The latter will be a particular boon to the deaf-blind and to those blind persons who work in noisy environments or in close proximity to others who might be distracted by frequent "spoken" answers.

Functional Barrier 3.4 DIFFICULTY IN USING OBJECTS IN THE WORK ENVIRONMENT

Any number of objects (and pieces of equipment) can interfere with job performance; many items may prove difficult to reach, difficult to manipulate, difficult to operate, or easy to damage. All workers face these problems at one time or another, and a branch of engineering--human factors engineering (Chapanis, 1968)--attempts to solve these and related problems. Handicapped workers often face problems greater than those faced by their nonhandicapped co-workers; frequently, they face major barriers in using objects in the work environment, while the nonhandicapped face none at all.

USING THESE STRATEGIES

The strategies discussed below can be used in many situations beyond those used to illustrate them. In applying these strategies, one should begin with a simple analysis, asking first what duties the worker must perform and what activities must be carried out to fulfill these duties. Next, those activities that prove particularly difficult should be identified. Some activities are crucial in executing job duties, while others are not. The former include activities that are inherent in the nature of the job--accountants must do arithmetic, mechanics must clean and gap spark plugs, and so on. The latter include activities that, while not inherent in the task, may be required in a particular job setting; for example, lifting heavy manuals is not the essence of computer programming, but it is often required. The first two strategies discussed below are appropriate to the latter class of activities, while the third and fourth strategies apply to the former class.

STRATEGIES FOR OVERCOMING THIS BARRIER

ALTERATIONS IN THE
WORK STATION

The setting in which a handicapped worker must perform is sometimes not conducive to accomplishing the job, even though the worker is capable of accomplishing it. Items may be placed out of reach or may be difficult to handle or manipulate. In the former case, an evaluation of the person's reach will enable objects to be placed where they are easily accessible. This is not simply a matter of adjusting the height of desks, benches, and shelves; the depth of shelves and benches, the distance from the edge of a bench to toolsacks, and the provision of adequate knee room for a person in a wheelchair to pull up fully to the bench or table are among other factors that must be considered.

Humanscale 1/2/3 (Diffrient, Tilley, & Bardagjy, 1974) provides detailed measurements showing the range of reach for persons in wheelchairs. Measurements are shown for persons of different heights relative to shelves and work surfaces; knee and foot clearances are also taken into consideration, as are passage widths, space needed in which to turn, toilet facilities, ramp design, floor coverings, and positioning of common items such as telephones. Similar data are provided for those who use canes or crutches, and environmental design tips are included for environments to be used by the blind or the deaf.

A related approach is to eliminate the need to reach an object in the usual way. Knorr and Hammond (1975), in their discussion of computer programmer training, describe how portions of manuals were photoenlarged and posted on classroom walls. Other reference works were propped up on lazy Susans so that pages could be turned with a mouthstick. Lazy Susans can be designed either for manual operation or for rotating in response to a switch.

Even if objects can be reached, they may prove too bulky or cumbersome to manipulate, or they may put excessive demands on fine-motor coordination. Such problems may be manifest in many ways, and solutions must be developed as each problem arises. Many solutions are little more than common sense:

1. Bulky, loose-leaf programming manuals, auto parts books, repair manuals, and the like can be broken up into several lighter volumes.

2. Rubber tubing, styrofoam, or rubber bands can be put around pencils, pens, screwdrivers, and the like to "enlarge" them. For those for whom these solutions are inadequate, holders are available to aid in gaining a firm grip; some attach directly to the hand if a satisfactory grip cannot otherwise be achieved.

3. Items such as staplers and writing paper that tend to "run away" when bumped by the uncoordinated can be fastened down using clamps, clipboards, etc. A ridge can be constructed around the edge of a workbench, table, or desk to restrain objects that cannot be fastened down either because it is physically difficult to do so, or because they must be picked up and used. Such a ridge would also be useful to any worker who has physical disabilities that make it difficult to retrieve items that have fallen from his or her desk or workbench.

EQUIPMENT MODIFICATIONS

Equipment may make demands on the worker that he/she cannot meet, but that are not inherently crucial to satisfactory performance. For example, many sewing machines are operated by treadles, but the critical factors in successful sewing should be positioning the cloth and moving it through the machine, not movement of the foot; treadles are used to control the needle speed only because they are convenient for most people. Motor speed can be controlled by switches operated by the knee, head, or mouth, and most equipment can be modified to permit this. (Of course, the reverse strategy will be needed for operation of machines with manual control by those persons with better foot than hand coordination.) Similarly, levers, handles, knobs, and buttons can be altered or repositioned to allow operation by those who could not formerly use them. Common alterations that may be needed include the following:

1. enlarged handles that can be more easily grasped;

2. protruding buttons to replace recessed ones for those persons with poor fine-motor coordination;

3. levers to replace knobs, thereby providing a better purchase for the weak;

4. push-pull or joystick controls to replace those that must be rotated, thus placing fewer demands on fine-motor coordination;

5. controls that are repositioned to place them within reach of an unparalyzed extremity; and

6. rings or extensions that are added to wheels or levers so that they can be moved more readily by an amputee with a hook.

In some cases, "equipment modification" may not mean the actual alteration of an existing piece of equipment, but the judicious selection of standard equipment or the addition of an auxiliary piece of equipment to an existing device. A careful review of equipment catalogs may reveal items that are lightweight, are shaped to allow an easy grasp, are automatic or semiautomatic, can be used with somewhat imprecise movements, have large or high-contrast markings, or for some other reason are well-suited for a particular person. Examples include electric staplers for the weak or poorly coordinated; electronic calculators with large displays for the visually impaired; automatic center punches that allow markings to be made on wood, metal, or other materials requiring use of only one hand; and office equipment in colors that take advantage of residual visual capabilities.

The use of auxiliary equipment may be illustrated in the case of telephone aids that allow normal telephone use by those whose movement capabilities are restricted. Semiautomatic dialers that dial numbers from preprogrammed cards are available for those lacking the dexterity needed to use the usual dial or pushbuttons. Similarly, headsets and mounts that hold handsets, which eliminate the need to pick up the receiver when making or receiving a call, are available. Modifications designed specifically to overcome sensory limitations are discussed in the section on barriers to communication. Devices that allow typewriter operation by persons with a variety of physical impairments are also discussed in the communications section; as pointed out there, the alliance of the keyboard and the computer opens a wide range of possibilities to the mentally able, physically impaired worker.

An example of the wedding of well-chosen standard equipment to an auxiliary apparatus is given by Hillam (1975). Hillam, a quadriplegic who pursues photography as a hobby, selected a fully-automatic 35mm single lens reflex camera equipped with a cable release and mounted it on his wheelchair so that the latter functions effectively as a tripod. This system eliminates the need for making most of the camera adjustments typically required for high quality photography.

SPECIAL TOOLS, PROSTHESES, AND OTHER AIDS

Sometimes job activities cannot be eliminated. In other cases, it may be undesirable to alter a work environment even if it is technically possible to do so. For example, many craftsmen move from bench to bench to complete various tasks. While it is easy to lower a bench for a person in a wheelchair, to do so poses an inconvenience for nonhandicapped co-workers; to lower one or two benches would restrict the handicapped worker to the one or two tasks performed at the lowered benches. In this case, adjustable wheelchairs could be provided that would raise the worker to the level of the benches (example given by A. G. Garris in Rehab Roundup, California Department of Vocational Rehabilitation, January 1974).

Similarly, if the handicapped worker must use tools designed for the nonhandicapped, special aids may be needed. Often, standard prostheses will be satisfactory; in other cases, more sophisticated appliances may be needed, for example, the "powered hook" (Hildred, 1973) that allows the operation of many standard tools (such as electric drills with "trigger" motor controls) by upper-limb amputees.

Other powered prostheses have been developed. While it is beyond the scope of this section to review this area in detail, the "Boston Arm," an EMG-controlled prosthesis (Mann, 1970, 1974), is particularly interesting. This device allows synergistic movements of the arms as well as more accurate limb positioning without visual guidance than is possible with traditional prostheses. Such a prosthesis should help to open jobs requiring two-hand coordination and delicacy in the placement of objects, particularly in jobs requiring the worker, for example, to reach for and operate controls while attending to gauges, meters, or other signals.

For those with partially paralyzed upper-limbs, recent advances in upper-limb orthoses (Hildred, 1973; Staros & Peizer, 1975) promise to provide lighter devices. These devices would more nearly match normal hand and finger motions, allowing the use of an increasing number of tools and equipment, particularly those items that require fine motor skills in the operation of controls.

Besides prostheses and orthoses, a wide variety of devices can be developed or employed to help the handicapped person succeed on the job. The number of situations that may arise, and the variety of solutions that may be developed, are so nearly limitless that it is not possible even to attempt to deal with them exhaustively. Following are a few examples:

1. bookstands with automatic page turners for the physically handicapped who need to make frequent reference to printed materials;

2. headwands, mouthsticks, pointers, and other probes for pushing buttons and similar controls by those who cannot reach them unaided;

3. devices similar to croupier sticks for drawing items toward the person who cannot reach them unaided;

4. devices used for lifting objects from high or low shelves such as the "E-Z Reacher," which allows objects to be grasped with opposed suction cups mounted on metal fingers at one end of a tube (the user adjusts the distance between the metal fingers by squeezing a trigger, thereby grasping or releasing objects); and

5. a dental aspirator and pump to draw off the liquid of a person with uncontrollable salivation, thereby preventing the saliva from falling on items in the work areas (example given by A. G. Garris in Rehab Roundup, California Department of Vocational Rehabilitation, May 1975).

JOB REDESIGN

The way in which job duties are performed or the activities assigned to particular workers in performing them are often determined as much by tradition as they are by what really needs to be done. There are at least three ways to overcome this problem: (1) reassign duties so that the strengths of each worker are capitalized upon and the importance of the worker's limitations are minimized--this can apply to the strengths and limitations of all workers, not just the handicapped; (2) alter the specific activities required so that the same duties are performed, but in a different way; and (3) entirely eliminate activities that are not really necessary for accomplishing the job. An example of each is given below. As with some of the strategies discussed earlier, the variety of situations and solutions is almost limitless; therefore, no attempt is made to be comprehensive.

REASSIGNMENT OF DUTIES

A machine operator who faces difficulties in fetching raw materials or in removing finished products to a central repository (because of blindness or an orthopedic impairment, for example) might be freed from these duties which, in turn, could be assigned to someone else. This other person could serve several machine operators, thereby increasing the number of products produced by freeing the skilled (and probably higher paid) employees from the need to leave their work stations.

ALTERATION OF WORK ACTIVITIES

Kidd (1971) provides an example of retarded workers who packed 100 items into cartons. As designed for nonretarded workers, this duty required counting to 100, which the retarded workers could not do. The activity was altered; instead of counting 100 objects, retarded workers simply placed an item in the carton with one hand while removing a token from another container with the other hand. The second container began with 100 tokens; when it became empty (which, of course, was when 100 items were placed in the carton), the entire procedure was repeated with the next carton.

ELIMINATION OF UNNECESSARY ACTIVITIES

Housman and Gentile (1972) provide an example showing how unnecessary activities can be eliminated. In this case, homebound clerks received calls reporting teacher illness and arranged for substitutes. Because the clerks were allowed to work at home, the activities associated with securing transportation to a central office were eliminated.

Barrier 4.0 Skills

Most nonhandicapped persons have access to a variety of vocational education opportunities that allow them to learn the skills, behaviors, and competencies needed to function on a job. They are able to obtain diplomas, certificates, or licenses that are prerequisite to certain vocations. Most persons with severe handicaps do not, for a number of reasons, profit from these vocational education opportunities and find it difficult to obtain adequate training to engage competitively in the economy. Adequate performance in a vocation presupposes several sets of skills other than the vocational, for example, independent living skills, basic education skills, and work adjustment skills.

Functional Barrier 4.1   LACK OF INDEPENDENT LIVING SKILLS

> In order for the handicapped worker to independently maintain himself/herself outside of a sheltered environment, the following kinds of skills must be mastered: self-bathing, using the toilet, clothing oneself, cooking, maintaining a household, taking care of emergencies, handling medical problems, handling money, caring for recreational needs, participating in a family, and so on. Handicapped persons often require intensive training in independent living skills as well as special training with mobility aids or prosthetic devices.

STRATEGIES FOR OVERCOMING THIS BARRIER

SHELTERED WORKSHOP TRAINING

Most sheltered workshops provide handicapped persons with training in independent daily living skills. For example, a four-month home economics training program, called Greentree School, was given to chronic schizophrenic women to help them cope with some of the everyday problems that they would encounter following discharge from the hospital. Women were trained in a variety of homemaking skills including selection and care of clothing and home furnishings, management of time and money, and child care (Central Hospital, Lakeland, Kentucky, 1971). The Sacramento Society for the Blind established an intensive five-week vocational course for young adults aged 15 to 20 years. The five-week course included part-time work experience, daily living instruction, and job placement (Laurence, 1973). The Hot Springs (Arkansas) Rehabilitation Center provided training in advanced living skills including driver education, recreational activities, vocational tutoring and evaluation, personal and social adjustment, and independent living (Rice & Milligan, 1973). Behavior modification techniques have been used to normalize personal appearance, speech, eating behaviors, and socialization, as well as to reduce deviant behaviors (Brickey, 1974).

OFF-CAMPUS OR HALFWAY HOUSE TRAINING

These settings utilize a more realistic environment to reinforce the mastery of independent living skills. For example, clients at the Sunland Training Center for Retarded Persons in Miami were given vocational and psychosocial evaluations; then a multidiscipline team developed independent rehabilitation plans for them that included independent living skills. After vocational and community orientations, clients received six weeks of basic on-campus vocational training and about 12 weeks of intensive off-campus training. Campus facilities included 30 job-training stations and a sheltered workshop; off campus were seven workshops and 20 on-the-job training programs (Cortazzo & Runnels, 1970).

HOMETRAINING

Most nonhandicapped workers learn independent living skills in the home. In many cases, handicapped persons also learn these skills in the home. Stewart (1971) has pointed out some problems of the severely handicapped deaf and the educational implications of these problems. Data on 106 deaf clients at the Hot Springs Rehabilitation Center in Arkansas show that the major impediments to rehabilitating these students are impoverished communication skills; behaviors that are inappropriate, inadequate, and impulsive; low levels of interest; and a lack of special services and trained staff to work with the severely handicapped deaf. As a result of these findings, one need that Stewart cites is better family interaction with young deaf children.

PUBLIC EDUCATION

As mainstreaming programs are developed, public education systems will be required to teach independent living skills to handicapped students. Luckey and Addison (1974) point out the necessity of redefining "education" to include the development and application of such skills as toilet training, dressing, grooming, and communication, particularly for severely retarded children.

JOB MODIFICATION   Another approach to this barrier has been to modify the job so that independent living skills are not required. Some work can be done at home, for example, telephone sales work or dispatching taxis or service vehicles. Zamochnick (1973) points out the problem of overtrained cerebral palsied individuals who cannot perform a professional job because of physical dependency. He suggests the development of jobs specifically for people in this category.

Functional Barrier 4.2   LACK OF BASIC EDUCATION SKILLS

The U.S. system of education currently operates so that those who learn the fastest are given the most education. It is unreasonable to expect handicapped persons to develop their maximum vocational potential in less time and with less assistance than that given nonhandicapped persons. In order to live independently in an industrialized society, every person must acquire certain fundamental knowledge. These skills, which are taught through formal education systems, are often unavailable to **severely handicapped** people because of their exclusion, for one reason or another, from the formal **education systems.**

STRATEGY FOR OVERCOMING THIS BARRIER

MAINSTREAMING   Mainstreaming is the practice of establishing procedures to assure that, to the maximum extent appropriate, handicapped persons are educated with persons who are not handicapped and that special classes, separate schooling, or other removal of handicapped persons from the regular educational environment occurs only when the nature and severity of the handicap precludes regular classroom education with the use of supplementary aids and services. For example, the North Central Institute's Program for Hearing Impaired Adults is mainstreaming deaf persons into ongoing occupational training programs. Instructional materials were developed to improve the vocabulary abilities of the deaf. Because signing had not been used as an instructional technique in many vocational areas, 8mm silent loop films with accompanying student workbooks, each consisting of about 100 words, were developed for a specific instructional area. The films, showing the sign and the printed word along with the equipment being identified, were developed for the following areas: printing, keypunching, account clerk, auto body, math, drafting, nurse's aide, business machines, blueprint reading, machine tools, filing, and sewing. Instruction is provided in orientation and mobility, personal and home management, and communications and work adjustment services. Students attend a 16-week prevocational phase, after which they enter occupational training programs, attend other institutions of higher education, obtain employment, or enter some other planned program (Lambert, 1975).

Functional Barrier 4.3 LACK OF WORK ADJUSTMENT ATTITUDES, SKILLS, AND CAPACITIES

Any worker must have a variety of work adjustment attitudes, skills, and capacities in order to succeed. The handicapped worker may have special problems because of restricted experience caused by the handicapping condition. Work adjustment attitudes, skills, and capacities include psychosocial skills (e.g., consistent and stable acceptable behavior; self-control over destructive, disruptive, inappropriate, or antisocial behavior); physical capacities (e.g., gross dexterity of hand and large arm muscles; good health; resistance to fatigue over time); critical performance skills (e.g., ability to follow directions or procedures; ability to adapt to changes in assignments, instructions, and procedures; ability to understand conversation, directions, and instructions as they relate to learning and performing assigned work); and work behavior and attitudes (e.g., an ability or willingness to listen to and make a genuine effort to follow through with supervisor instructions, suggestions, and directives; the desire and effort to work; a willingness to work at a task until it is completed).

STRATEGIES FOR OVERCOMING THIS BARRIER

WORK SIMULATION, CONDITIONING, AND EXPERIENCE

Most rehabilitation and training programs for the severely handicapped include work simulation, work conditioning training, or actual work experience. These methods are designed to allow the student to practice working, with some sort of incentive as payment, in order to build up work tolerance. For example, the Work Experience Center operated by the St. Louis Jewish Employment and Vocational Service has developed a reality-oriented habilitation workshop designed for those who have never known the world of work. In order to help prepare clients for community living, the habilitation workshop attempts to give clients job-site as well as workshop experience (Bitter & Bolanovitch, 1966). As a second example, Fountain House in New York established a halfway house for deaf psychiatric patients (Bean & Beard, 1975). Deaf persons referred from the Rockland State Hospital are provided a variety of vocational opportunities. The Temporary Employment Placement Program provides semi-sheltered community employment so that clients can learn good work habits and become acclimated to the world of work before leaving the house. Jackson (1971) reported a pilot project in Austin, Texas, that was designed to serve severely retarded persons who were ineligible for regular vocational rehabilitation programs. Fifteen severely retarded adults were first extended sheltered workshop employment opportunities, including personal-social adjustment training, work adjustment training, and on-the-job training in assembly work; they were then offered community living services at two halfway houses. During the pilot program's first five months, occupancy rate was nearly 100%; monthly earnings per client ranged from $6 to $25, with an average of $8. Trybus and Lacks (1972) reported that the Behavioral Training Unit of the Work Experience Center in St. Louis, mentioned above, used operant-based behavior modification techniques in a project designed to teach work adjustment skills to 19 moderately to severely retarded adolescents who were unable to work in a sheltered workshop because of their low productivity and unmanageable behavior problems. The group training used a token system, a set of cuing lights, and such reinforcers as food, money, break time, and attention from supervisors. The operant techniques were successful in reversing work-interfering behaviors and in increasing productivity. It appeared that the controlled environment needed to be maintained for the improved behavior and performance to persist.

SUPPORTIVE COUNSELING   Another widespread technique used to overcome this barrier is supportive counseling. An
example is the Young Adult Institute and Workshop of New York City, which provided an
Adjustment Center for mentally retarded and otherwise disadvantaged persons over the age
of 16. Most of the students served were multiply handicapped and were not yet in job
training programs. The Adjustment Center provided small group counseling sessions in
problem solving and change, social skills, communication skills, and employment skills.
Individual counseling was provided as needed (Ames, 1970).

Functional Barrier 4.4 LACK OF VOCATIONAL SKILL DEVELOPMENT

Vocational training programs vary widely in scope, methods, the extent to which research is integrated into programming procedures, the extent to which business, labor, and industry are involved, and the training environment. Vocational skill, commensurate with the individual handicapped worker's goals and potential, is a prerequisite to job placement; thus, it can be an important barrier to employment and should be addressed.

STRATEGIES FOR OVERCOMING THIS BARRIER

INDIVIDUALIZED PROGRAMMED INSTRUCTION

Most programs have some sort of individualized instruction. However, improvements in this area are suggested. Based on the findings of a state-wide assessment in Illinois, Szoke (1974) proposed the need for in-depth vocational assessment of handicapped students and for individualized programmed instructional materials. Szoke contends that "special needs" students can achieve the occupational competency of nonhandicapped students, though perhaps at a slower rate or with a different method.

PARAPROFESSIONAL TUTORS

The paraprofessional role usually supplements the more formal aspects of vocational programming. The paraprofessional may be assigned the role of presenting content; supplying active tutorial assistance to individuals or small groups of students; serving a monitorial function to help maintain discipline and attention in a crowded or shared-teacher classroom or instructional setting; or serving as a practice agent to improve the value and facilitate the administration of learning activities. Craighead and Mercatoris (1973) have reported several projects that employ the mentally retarded as tutors. Generally, the mentally retarded tutors served as reinforcers for a specific target behavior in an experimental setting. Whether or not these paraprofessionals can work without extensive supervision, and thus conserve staff time, remains to be seen. Craighead and Mercatoris concluded, however, that their mentally retarded students exhibited the same learning curves when trained by retardates as when trained by staff, and that the major value of the programs accrued to the tutor.

MODELING

One of the fundamental means by which new modes of behavior are acquired and existing patterns are modified entails modeling and vicarious processes. Research has demonstrated that virtually all learning phenomena resulting from direct experiences can occur on a vicarious basis through observation of others' behavior and the consequences of that behavior (Bandura, 1965). Thus, to illustrate, one can acquire intricate new learning merely by observing the performances of appropriate models; emotional responses can be conditioned through observation of the responses of persons undergoing emotional experiences; and the expression of well-learned responses can be enhanced and taught through the actions of influential models. Burleson (1973) reported the use of these techniques with a 38-year-old retarded, legally blind male. Institutionalized for 26 years, the client had previously avoided social interactions and refused teaching services. The modeling technique, used to reduce his anxiety and enable him to learn new skills, emphasized the primary sense modalities, particularly audition and tactile perception. Use of the modeling technique enabled the client to function at a significantly higher level, to improve his self-concept and social skills, and to attain employment in the community.

OPERANT BEHAVIOR MODIFICATION

Many programs are using behavior modification techniques, particularly those dealing with the severely mentally retarded and the mutiply handicapped. The University of Oregon's

University Affiliated Facility and Rehabilitation Research and Training Center in Mental Retardation is developing specialized training programs for the severely and profoundly retarded in an effort to reduce the amount of time needed to acquire vocational skills and improve productivity in the work place. This behavior-oriented program has developed methods of training retarded persons to discriminate and then attend to relevant dimensions of the task through a series of simple-to-difficult discriminations. Practical applications have been made to such relatively complex tasks as assembling bicycle parts. Various approaches have emphasized diversifying the supervisor instructions (Bellamy, 1976), enriching the training (Gold, 1972), giving verbal instructions to correct errors during the original learning (Gold & Barclay, 1973), determining the effects of a realistic working environment on base rates of performance (Brickey, 1974), and so on. Yarbrough (1972) reports an automated system that was used to monitor behaviors in a sheltered workshop. Tools wired to an operant programming and recording apparatus were used to transduce behaviors; the task consisted of constructing electronic equipment. As a result of this monitoring technique, it was reported that a great deal of objective information was available to help the supervisor measure the client's progress.

WORK EXPERIENCE   Work experience obtained on the job is a very widespread method used to increase vocational skills. The techniques vary from simulated work experience in a sheltered workshop to on-the-job training conducted by the business or industry itself. An example is the program that was used by Abilities, Inc. of Florida (1966). Patterned after a similar organization located in Albertson, New York, Abilities, Inc. of Florida provided employment in a competitive work environment in the manufacture of electronic equipment, direct mail advertising, and printing. Contracts for work at the center were secured with private businesses. Generally, applicants were required to work at the center, although part of the direct mail operation was handled by homebound employees. The ages of employees ranged from 22 to over 60. Employees had a wide variety of physical impairments (e.g., mental retardation, amputation, polio, arthritis, and congenital abnormalities). Employees worked a standard work day and received wages and benefits comparable to prevailing local rates. Some of the jobs done were soldering, fabrication, and assembly of electronic equipment; operation of mechanical addressing and folding equipment; compilation of mailing lists; operation of letterset and offset presses; and binding, platemaking, and layout.

In an effort to reflect current employer needs and trends in competitive employment, the center's training programs were reviewed by experts in industry, government, and education. Between 1960 and 1966, Abilities, Inc. trained approximately 200 people, most of whom had been referred by state vocational rehabilitation agencies. About one-third of them were rehabilitated, and the remainder were referred to sheltered workshops and other agencies.

Another example of work experience obtained on the job is the Projects with Industry program funded by the Social and Rehabilitation Service. This placement-oriented program offers to the disabled employment opportunities ranging from manual labor to professional work in over 500 firms. Rehabilitation agencies and business firms implementing the program are Cole National Corporation; International Business Machines Corporation; MacDonald Training Center in Tampa, Florida; the Easter Seal Goodwill Industries Rehabilitation Center in New Haven, Connecticut; the Chicago Jewish Vocational Services; the Human Resources Center in Albertson, New York; and Fountain House in New York City. During the latter half of 1973, 62% of the 1,724 disabled persons served were placed on jobs. The cost of each placement was $1,000, as opposed to $2,137 in the state/federal vocational rehabilitation program.

Still another example of on-the-job work experience is a three-year demonstration project conducted by the Special School District of St. Louis County (the Missouri State Division of Vocational Rehabilitation) and the St. Louis Jewish Employment and Vocational Service. The program trained clients between 16 and 21 years of age with IQs ranging from 40 to 65. Clients entered a five-phase program including (1) general evaluation and vocational adjustment (intramural), (2) job-site evaluation and vocational adjustment (extramural), (3) specific job preparation and/or occupational training, (4) job placement and tryout, and (5) employment and follow-up. As a result of this project, staff stressed the need for extramural programming that includes community and industrial resources.

DRUG THERAPY

For seriously emotionally disturbed workers, clinical control of symptoms and enhanced work performance is achieved by the use of appropriate drug therapy. Chacon, Harper, and Harvey (1972) reported a study in which the work performance of 34 male chronic schizophrenics was tested over a 12-week period to compare the effects of two drugs, chlorpromazine and fluenazine decanoate, and a placebo. Results showed a significant increase in performance on a complex task when the subjects were receiving fluenazine decanoate.

SYSTEMS APPROACH

Banathy (1973) defined a system as an interacting group of entities forming an organized whole. More specifically, it is a deliberately designed synthetic entity made up of diverse but interdependent components that interact and are united according to some organizing idea, plan, or central principle. A system becomes more than the aggregate of its components. Generally, the first step in establishing a system is to clearly define the output. In most cases, the output for vocational training and placement programs for severely handicapped persons is employability of the handicapped person. Employability can be defined at the outset as those behaviors one wishes to see expressed at the end of the program. Next, the person is evaluated to see what behaviors she/he is lacking and then a step-by-step course is outlined for the client to follow to reach the desired ends. Feedback loops are built into the system so that the course can be corrected, and the process is continued until the outcome is reached. Emphasis is placed on defining all needed components to achieve the desired outcomes, and each component's function is articulated within the whole system.

An example of the systems approach applied to the vocational training and placement of the severely handicapped is that of the San Antonio Goodwill Rehabilitation Services' Competency Model Program (Lippman & Porter, 1976). Employability, designated as the ultimate goal for all clients, was defined as concrete, observable behaviors in three components: (1) physical/sensory capabilities; (2) social/emotional characteristics; and (3) functional education skills. Competency in these areas was established in terms of local norms required for the San Antonio community. Clients were identified as handicapped when there was an absence of required competencies. Proficiency levels were established for each desirable behavior on a scale from 1 to 5. Level 1 indicated an absence of the desired skill or behavior, and level 5 indicated proficiency in the desired skill or behavior. Task analyses were undertaken to determine the method to be used to attain competency in desired behaviors for each individual. Activities were sequenced to achieve the desired behaviors with frequent individual monitoring to determine progress toward mastery. Documentation of progress was a part of the rehabilitation process.

An example of the systems approach applied to curriculum materials for the severely handicapped is a curriculum guide to seven para-cosmetologist occupations for the physically handicapped. The guide was prepared by the UCLA Division of Vocational Education in cooperation with the Bureau of Industrial Education and the California State Department of Education. Behavioral objectives are presented for each identified task and are written in a format that stresses clarity. The information to be presented, the desired student performance, and the final standard performance are all identified. Estimated instructional hours varied from 75 to 500 for each of the occupations (University of California at Los Angeles, 1971).

REORGANIZATION OF PROGRAMS INTO MULTIAGENCY CENTERS

Greenleigh Associates (1969) proposed a model program to serve handicapped people who are potentially employable. The program would include training stipends, guaranteed job placement in manpower training programs, flexible training techniques, sheltered workshops for work evaluation, and work adjustment and pre-employment training. Greenleigh Associates recommended that existing agencies be reorganized into multiagency centers. Their recommendation was based on the fact that many agencies do not have the resources to predict the changing labor market or the range of medical, social, and financial capabilities necessary to serve the handicapped effectively.

occupational division tables

DESCRIPTION OF TABLES   This section of the handbook contains 63 tables based on the occupational divisions in the fourth edition of the Dictionary of Occupational Titles (DOT) and on a survey conducted as part of the VOTAP project. Figure 1 shows a sample table and explains each entry. The two entries at the top give the code number and name of the occupational division and discuss the jobs included in it.

The list of "Jobs Held by Handicapped Workers" came from the 169 VOTAP survey respondents. Table entries should not be taken as a complete compilation of jobs performed by the handicapped; most readers probably know of persons succeeding at jobs not included on these lists. The purpose of these lists, taken together, is to document that a wide variety of jobs are within reach of severely handicapped people, and to encourage the exploration of a wide variety of jobs by the handicapped person, the counselor, and the trainer. The fact that a job is not listed does not imply that it should not be considered; such an implication would be contrary to the purpose for which these lists are intended.

The "Other Jobs in This Division" shows the variety of related jobs that a handicapped person might like to investigate. No doubt many are already being performed by handicapped persons who were not known to VOTAP survey respondents. In any case, those with interests and abilities in fields specified by these divisions may find these jobs well worth exploring.

"Opening Jobs in This Division" discusses the barriers that a handicapped person may face in securing training or placement. Strategies for overcoming these barriers are treated in a previous section of this handbook. The fact that a barrier is mentioned in this entry does not imply that it will be faced by every handicapped person seeking a job in that division. The seriousness of the barriers mentioned depends on the individual's handicapping condition, the building in which the work is to be performed, the feelings and conduct of co-workers, the adroitness of the handicapped person in making himself or herself understood or in putting others at ease, and a host of other factors unique to the specific situation.

To summarize, the purpose of the tables that follow is to provide a sample of the wide variety of jobs that handicapped people now hold; to point out similar jobs for investigation by the handicapped person or by a professional working with that person; and to direct attention to strategies that may be used to overcome certain barriers.

FINDING JOBS   This handbook can be used to help identify jobs for the severely handicapped. The essential steps are to determine (1) behavioral repertoire, (2) interests and vocational aspirations, (3) local job possibilities, (4) job demands to which the handicapped person must be capable of responding, and (5) the strategy that is necessary to reinforce, augment, or supplement the person in order to manage her or his deficiency.

The idea is not simply to match the person and the occupation. The role of the training or placement officer is to be more than a trainer, counselor, or job finder. He or she becomes a strategist with many possible options, for example, to select jobs in which the client's deficiency is irrelevant, to provide special training, to enhance the person's capabilities with an assistive device, and to reengineer the job. The occupational division tables in this handbook will give the training or placement officer a very good idea of the types of jobs that the severely handicapped are presently performing. They also describe the most likely problems and some strategies that can be used to overcome the problems.

The following example, based on the Peterson and Jones (1976) approach, illustrates how steps 1 through 5 described above might be achieved.

1. Prepare a client profile that contains three types of summary information.

    a. Job activities for which the client has been trained, with an estimate of her or his performance on each of them.

    b. Personal characteristics of the client as determined by personal observation, tests and evaluations, work samples, and so on.

    c. Client interests and estimates of motivation for employment. Client and parent interests and ambitions, if realistic, should play an important part in placing the clients in a suitable job.

2. Identify patterns of job ability from the client's profile, determining patterns of strengths and weaknesses in both job activities and personal characteristics. Since the client may have been exposed to a wide variety of job activities in training rather than being trained for a given job, identifying a job-related pattern may be difficult.

3. Compare client patterns with the jobs described in the tables; seek jobs in which the client's strengths will be an asset and her or his weaknesses will not cause problems, or seek jobs in which weaknesses may be reduced by more specific job training. Job orientation and on-the-job training may substantially contribute to the client's effectiveness.

4. When one or more potential jobs have been identified, systematically review the client's capabilities, limitations, and interests with a specific job in mind. Begin with the job that seems to match the client's patterns most closely. Ask the following kinds of questions:

    o Where does the client match the job, and what does she or he lack most?

    o Are the deficiencies critical to probable job success?

    o Will the employer be likely to accept the client?

5. Determine whether some or all of these deficiencies can be made up in some way. Refer to the barriers section of this handbook for possible strategies.

6. Discuss the barriers and strategies with your client to determine how he or she would like to approach management of the barriers. Depending on the client's suggestions, you might meet with employers, state rehabilitation counselors, special education counselors, or other resource people to develop a strategy for successfully placing your client.

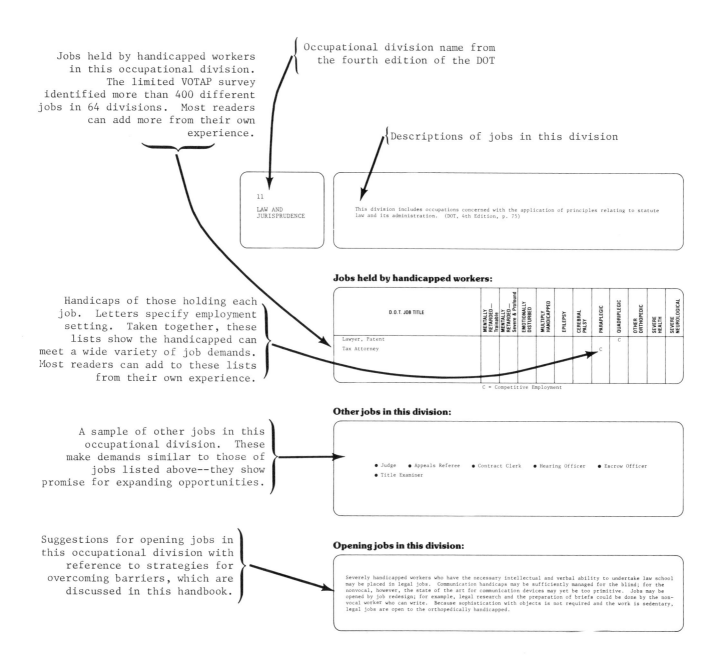

Jobs held by handicapped workers
in this occupational division.
The limited VOTAP survey
identified more than 400 different
jobs in 64 divisions. Most readers
can add more from their own
experience.

Occupational division name from
the fourth edition of the DOT

Descriptions of jobs in this division

11

LAW AND
JURISPRUDENCE

This division includes occupations concerned with the application of principles relating to statute law and its administration. (DOT, 4th Edition, p. 75)

Jobs held by handicapped workers:

Handicaps of those holding each
job. Letters specify employment
setting. Taken together, these
lists show the handicapped can
meet a wide variety of job demands.
Most readers can add to these lists
from their own experience.

D.O.T. JOB TITLE	MENTALLY RETARDED— Trainable	MENTALLY RETARDED— Severe & Profound	EMOTIONALLY DISTURBED	MULTIPLY HANDICAPPED	EPILEPSY	CEREBRAL PALSY	PARAPLEGIC	QUADRIPLEGIC	OTHER ORTHOPEDIC	SEVERE HEALTH	SEVERE NEUROLOGICAL
Lawyer, Patent								C			
Tax Attorney							C				

C = Competitive Employment

Other jobs in this division:

A sample of other jobs in this
occupational division. These
make demands similar to those of
jobs listed above--they show
promise for expanding opportunities.

● Judge   ● Appeals Referee   ● Contract Clerk   ● Hearing Officer   ● Escrow Officer
● Title Examiner

Opening jobs in this division:

Suggestions for opening jobs in
this occupational division with
reference to strategies for
overcoming barriers, which are
discussed in this handbook.

Severely handicapped workers who have the necessary intellectual and verbal ability to undertake law school may be placed in legal jobs. Communication handicaps may be sufficiently managed for the blind; for the nonvocal, however, the state of the art for communication devices may yet be too primitive. Jobs may be opened by job redesign; for example, legal research and the preparation of briefs could be done by the non-vocal worker who can write. Because sophistication with objects is not required and the work is sedentary, legal jobs are open to the orthopedically handicapped.

Figure 1. Occupational Division Table

51

This division includes occupations concerned with the practical application of physical laws and principles of engineering and/or architecture for the development and utilization of machines, materials, instruments, structures, processes, and services. Typical specializations are research, design, construction, testing, procurement, production, operations, and sales. Also includes preparation of drawings, specifications, and cost estimates, and participation in verification tests. (DOT, 4th Edition, p. 15)

Jobs held by handicapped workers:

D.O.T. JOB TITLE	MENTALLY RETARDED—Trainable	MENTALLY RETARDED—Severe & Profound	EMOTIONALLY DISTURBED	MULTIPLY HANDICAPPED	EPILEPSY	CEREBRAL PALSY	PARAPLEGIC	QUADRIPLEGIC	OTHER ORTHOPEDIC	SEVERE HEALTH	SEVERE NEUROLOGICAL
Electrical Engineer										C	
Civil Engineer								C			
Tool Designer							C				
Petroleum Engineer								C			
Photographic Engineer								C	C		
Systems Analyst, Electronic Data Processing			C								
Engineering Assistant, Mechanical Equipment								C			
Drafter, Architectural					C			C			
Drafter, Mechanical								C			
Auto-Design Detailer			C								
Electronics Technician									C	C	

C = Competitive Employment

Other jobs in this division:

- Engineer of System Development
- Protection Engineer
- Commercial Engineer
- Drafter, Civil
- Plant Engineer
- Air Analyst
- Packaging Engineer
- Editor, Map
- Drafter, Assistant
- Mining Engineer
- Supervisor, Estimator and Drafter (light, heat, & power)

Opening jobs in this division:

The variety of severely handicapped persons presently holding jobs in this occupational division suggests that many handicaps can be successfully managed. An inability to apply technical knowledge and the demands of an extensive mainstreamed education will prohibit many handicapped workers from entering these jobs. A redesigned work place and special mobility equipment or tools may be helpful.

<table>
<tr><td rowspan="2">02</td></tr>
</table>

02	This division includes occupations concerned with research pertaining to the physical universe, and the application of established mathematical and scientific laws and principles to specific problems and situations. (DOT, 4th Edition, p. 37)
MATHEMATICS AND PHYSICAL SCIENCES	

Jobs held by handicapped workers:

D.O.T. JOB TITLE	MENTALLY RETARDED— Trainable	MENTALLY RETARDED— Severe & Profound	EMOTIONALLY DISTURBED	MULTIPLY HANDICAPPED	EPILEPSY	CEREBRAL PALSY	PARAPLEGIC	QUADRIPLEGIC	OTHER ORTHOPEDIC	SEVERE HEALTH	SEVERE NEUROLOGICAL
Financial Analyst									C		
Programmer, Business			C					C			
Programmer, Engineering and Scientific								C			
Statistician, Mathematical									C		
Project Manager, Environmental Research							C				

C = Competitive Employment

Other jobs in this division:

- Mathematician
- Chemist
- Physicist
- Geologist
- Laboratory Tester
- Geographer
- Environmental Analyst

Opening jobs in this division:

Mobility aids, communication devices, and specially designed work stations will be likely means of opening jobs to handicapped persons with the requisite intellectual capacity for these jobs. It is unlikely that sufficient training will be available outside the formal education system; thus, handicapped workers should be capable of being mainstreamed into formal education systems.

04

LIFE SCIENCES

This division includes occupations concerned with research to increase basic knowledge of living organisms, including humans, and the practical application of biological and behavioral theories. (DOT, 4th Edition, p. 44)

Jobs held by handicapped workers:

D.O.T. JOB TITLE	MENTALLY RETARDED—Trainable	MENTALLY RETARDED—Severe & Profound	EMOTIONALLY DISTURBED	MULTIPLY HANDICAPPED	EPILEPSY	CEREBRAL PALSY	PARAPLEGIC	QUADRIPLEGIC	OTHER ORTHOPEDIC	SEVERE HEALTH	SEVERE NEUROLOGICAL
Counselor								C	C	C	
Horticulturalist				C							
Microbiologist							C	C			
Histopathologist							C				

C = Competitive Employment

Other jobs in this division:

- Psychologist
- Director of Guidance in Public Schools
- Biochemist
- Botanist
- Pharmacologist

Opening jobs in this division:

Jobs in this occupational division demand the intellectual capabilities required for research. In addition, many require the ability to do precision work with objects. For workers who have the intellectual ability but are handicapped by communication or mobility barriers, special tools or devices tailored to their needs may need to be utilized, adapted, or erected. Job restructuring may minimize the need to manipulate objects by having someone else do these tasks. Special training may be useful in augmenting skills.

07
MEDICINE AND HEALTH

This division includes occupations concerned with the health care of humans or animals in the fields of medicine, surgery, and dentistry; and in related patient-care areas, such as nursing, therapy, dietetics, prosthetics, rehabilitation, and pharmacy. Also included are occupations in sanitation, environmental and public health, and in laboratories and other health facilities. Many occupations in this category require licensing or registration to practice or use a specific title. (DOT, 4th Edition, p. 52)

Jobs held by handicapped workers:

D.O.T. JOB TITLE	MENTALLY RETARDED—Trainable	MENTALLY RETARDED—Severe & Profound	EMOTIONALLY DISTURBED	MULTIPLY HANDICAPPED	EPILEPSY	CEREBRAL PALSY	PARAPLEGIC	QUADRIPLEGIC	OTHER ORTHOPEDIC	SEVERE HEALTH	SEVERE NEUROLOGICAL
Psychiatrist								C			
Chemistry Technologist			C								
Medical Laboratory Technician										C	
Medical Technologist			C				C				
Medical Assistant			C								
Physical Therapist										C	

C = Competitive Employment

Other jobs in this division:

- Anesthesiologist
- Gynecologist
- Pediatrician
- Dentist
- Orthodontist
- Veterinarian
- Nurse, General Duty
- Speech Pathologist
- Art Therapist
- Public Health Educator
- Dental Hygienist
- Dental Assistant
- Podiatrist

Opening jobs in this division:

Almost all jobs in this division require high intellectual ability and extensive academic preparation. For most of these jobs, preparation is probably unavailable except through mainstream programs. Sensory and motor demands vary widely. Increasingly sophisticated aids and workstation redesign techniques may be expected to open more jobs in this division. Still, the key to success in this division, with its wide variety of demands, is to select a job compatible with the individual's capabilities.

09
EDUCATION

This division includes occupations in education concerned with research, administration, and teaching. Includes occupations in the administration of Federal, State, and private programs for which a background in education is required. Includes aids who assist classroom teachers by instructing sections of classes, coaching individual pupils, and grading papers, but excludes aides where educational preparation is not specific and tasks of jobs include various clerical or service tasks. Classroom aide occupations in primary and secondary schools are included in Group 149. Occupations concerned with teaching dramatics, dancing, music, athletics, games of mental skill, e.g., bridge and chess, and sports, other than in primary and secondary schools, are included in appropriate groups under Division 15. Occupations concerned with student and teacher personnel work and vocational guidance are included in Groups 045 and 166. Administrative occupations which do not require a background of education are included in groups under Division 16. (DOT, 4th Edition, p. 65)

Jobs held by handicapped workers:

D.O.T. JOB TITLE	MENTALLY RETARDED—Trainable	MENTALLY RETARDED—Severe & Profound	EMOTIONALLY DISTURBED	MULTIPLY HANDICAPPED	EPILEPSY	CEREBRAL PALSY	PARAPLEGIC	QUADRIPLEGIC	OTHER ORTHOPEDIC	SEVERE HEALTH	SEVERE NEUROLOGICAL
Faculty Member, College or University								C			
Teacher, Secondary School							C	C			

C = Competitive Employment

Other jobs in this division:

- Director of Admissions
- Teacher, Industrial Arts
- Teacher, Blind
- Teacher, Deaf
- Home Economist
- Consultant, Education
- Teacher, Adult Education
- Teacher Aide
- Athletic Director

Opening jobs in this division:

These jobs require the handicapped worker to possess high intellectual capability, the ability to communicate both vocally and in writing, and at least a bachelor's degree in an appropriate subject area. Severe barriers to the handicapped worker are communication handicaps, public attitudes, and difficulty in obtaining an appropriate public education. Many job areas do not require facility with objects or demand high-level mobility.

This division includes occupations concerned with library and archival sciences, including public and private libraries and archives, and with maintaining museums, galleries, and related exhibits. (DOT, 4th Edition, p. 72)

Jobs held by handicapped workers:

D.O.T. JOB TITLE	MENTALLY RETARDED—Trainable	MENTALLY RETARDED—Severe & Profound	EMOTIONALLY DISTURBED	MULTIPLY HANDICAPPED	EPILEPSY	CEREBRAL PALSY	PARAPLEGIC	QUADRIPLEGIC	OTHER ORTHOPEDIC	SEVERE HEALTH	SEVERE NEUROLOGICAL
Curator						C					

C = Competitive Employment

Other jobs in this division:

- Paintings Restorer
- Information Scientist
- Research Worker, Encyclopedia
- Research Assistant

Opening jobs in this division:

All jobs in this division require sophistication in dealing with information. The setting in which work is carried out will cause great variation in physical demands. Thus, architectural barrier removal and workplace redesign are especially critical in opening jobs in this division.

11	This division includes occupations concerned with the application of principles relating to statute law and its administration. (DOT, 4th Edition, p. 75)
LAW AND JURISPRUDENCE	

Jobs held by handicapped workers:

D.O.T. JOB TITLE	MENTALLY RETARDED— Trainable	MENTALLY RETARDED— Severe & Profound	EMOTIONALLY DISTURBED	MULTIPLY HANDICAPPED	EPILEPSY	CEREBRAL PALSY	PARAPLEGIC	QUADRIPLEGIC	OTHER ORTHOPEDIC	SEVERE HEALTH	SEVERE NEUROLOGICAL
Lawyer, Patent								C			
Tax Attorney							C				

C = Competitive Employment

Other jobs in this division:

- Judge
- Appeals Referee
- Contract Clerk
- Hearing Officer
- Escrow Officer
- Title Examiner

Opening jobs in this division:

Severely handicapped workers who have the necessary intellectual and verbal ability to undertake law school may be placed in legal jobs. Communication handicaps may be sufficiently managed for the blind; for the nonvocal, however, the state of the art for communication devices may yet be too primitive. Jobs may be opened by job redesign; for example, legal research and the preparation of briefs could be done by the nonvocal worker who can write. Because sophistication with objects is not required and the work is sedentary, legal jobs are open to the orthopedically handicapped.

<table>
<tr><td>13
WRITING</td><td>This division includes occupations concerned with reporting, editing, promoting, and interpreting ideas and facts in written form. Occupations concerned with translating and interpreting written and spoken words from one language to another are also included in this division. (DOT, 4th Edition, p. 77)</td></tr>
</table>

Jobs held by handicapped workers:

D.O.T. JOB TITLE	MENTALLY RETARDED— Trainable	MENTALLY RETARDED— Severe & Profound	EMOTIONALLY DISTURBED	MULTIPLY HANDICAPPED	EPILEPSY	CEREBRAL PALSY	PARAPLEGIC	QUADRIPLEGIC	OTHER ORTHOPEDIC	SEVERE HEALTH	SEVERE NEUROLOGICAL
Editor, Publications								C			
Reporter						C		C			

C = Competitive Employment

Other jobs in this division:

- Columnist/Commentator
- Copy Writer
- Critic
- Screen Writer
- Newscaster
- Script Reader
- Editor, Newspaper
- Interpreter
- Translator

Opening jobs in this division:

Major barriers to handicapped workers in this division include restricted mobility (required to do necessary research), communication barriers (inability to write), and difficulties in obtaining sufficient education for skill development. Persons who have writing skills may be able to depend upon others to gather information. Writing devices could be utilized for those unable to write, and mobility devices could be utilized where possible.

14
ART

This division includes occupations concerned with integrating personal expression, knowledge of subject matter, and art concepts, techniques, and processes to develop ideas and create environments, products, and art works which elicit an emotional or esthetic response. Occupations concerned with teaching are included in Groups 091, 092, and 097. Occupations in performing arts are included in Groups 150, 151, and 152. Occupations in art museums are included in Group 102. (DOT, 4th Edition, p. 80)

Jobs held by handicapped workers:

D.O.T. JOB TITLE	MENTALLY RETARDED— Trainable	MENTALLY RETARDED— Severe & Profound	EMOTIONALLY DISTURBED	MULTIPLY HANDICAPPED	EPILEPSY	CEREBRAL PALSY	PARAPLEGIC	QUADRIPLEGIC	OTHER ORTHOPEDIC	SEVERE HEALTH	SEVERE NEUROLOGICAL
Graphic Designer			C								
Illustrator				C						C	

C = Competitive Employment

Other jobs in this division:

● Cartoonist ● Fashion Artist ● Clothes Designer ● Floral Designer ● Painter ● Sculptor
● Photographer

Opening jobs in this division:

Handicapped and nonhandicapped persons who do not possess artistic talent will be excluded from jobs in this division. Severely handicapped persons who have artistic capabilities may find employment if special tools and devices are developed to help them work in their mediums or if a nontraditional approach is used, such as used by mouth and foot artists. In either case, slow production speed may be a problem. In some cases work places may have to be redesigned to accommodate specific needs. Special training may augment skills.

15

ENTERTAINMENT
AND RECREATION

This division includes occupations concerned with amusing, diverting, or informing others by such means as sound or physical movement. Includes teaching these skills (except occupations in primary, secondary, and vocational schools which are included in Groups 091, 092, and 097). (DOT, 4th Edition, p. 85)

Jobs held by handicapped workers:

D.O.T. JOB TITLE	MENTALLY RETARDED—Trainable	MENTALLY RETARDED—Severe & Profound	EMOTIONALLY DISTURBED	MULTIPLY HANDICAPPED	EPILEPSY	CEREBRAL PALSY	PARAPLEGIC	QUADRIPLEGIC	OTHER ORTHOPEDIC	SEVERE HEALTH	SEVERE NEUROLOGICAL
Announcer							C				
Disc Jockey									C		

C = Competitive Employment

Other jobs in this division:

- Dramatic Coach
- Teacher, Drama
- Actor
- Narrator
- Musician, Instrumental
- Singer
- Arranger
- Head Coach
- Athletic Trainer
- Umpire
- Dancer

Opening jobs in this division:

Jobs in this division vary widely in their requirements. Some, such as radio announcing, make few physical demands, but require a highly verbal worker with a pleasant, well-articulated voice. Physical modifications to overcome architectural or work station barriers should almost always be possible. Other jobs, for example, dancing and instrumental music, make unavoidable physical demands but practically none in the areas of voice quality and articulation. The key here is careful guidance to help the person find a suitable job in entertainment.

16

ADMINISTRATIVE
SPECIALIZATIONS

This division includes occupations concerned with specialized administrative and managerial functions which are common to many types of organizations. (Managerial occupations which are peculiar to one or a few related types of organizations are included in Division 18). In general, occupations included in the group listed below demand a knowledge of a particular function rather than a knowledge of the operations of an organization included in Division 18. Includes occupations which involve the more routine nonclerical duties or a combination of clerical and administrative work. Occupations involving clerical work exclusively in these fields are not included. (DOT, 4th Edition, p. 91)

Jobs held by handicapped workers:

D.O.T. JOB TITLE	MENTALLY RETARDED—Trainable	MENTALLY RETARDED—Severe & Profound	EMOTIONALLY DISTURBED	MULTIPLY HANDICAPPED	EPILEPSY	CEREBRAL PALSY	PARAPLEGIC	QUADRIPLEGIC	OTHER ORTHOPEDIC	SEVERE HEALTH	SEVERE NEUROLOGICAL
Employment Interviewer							C	C			
Accountant			C		C				C	C	
Underwriter								C			

Other jobs in this division:

- Revenue Agent
- Auditors
- Credit Counselor
- Management Analyst
- Buyer
- Purchasing Agent
- Field Representative
- Public-Relations Representative
- Recruiter
- Inspector, Building
- Claim Examiner
- Administrative Assistant
- Administrative Secretary
- Underwriter

Opening jobs in this division:

Critical barriers for the handicapped worker in these jobs are public attitudes, communication handicaps, lack of skill and, in some cases, lack of mobility. Considerable aptitude is required in handling data and people; thus, the retarded would be excluded in most cases. Mobility handicaps are probably manageable in most of these jobs. These jobs would be difficult for the nonvocal unless information could be efficiently communicated by some other means. These jobs would also be difficult for persons with severe cosmetic handicaps.

<table>
<tr><td rowspan="2">18</td><td rowspan="6">This division includes managerial occupations which require a knowledge of the management and operations of an organization, rather than a scientific, technical, or administrative specialty. Generally speaking, these are 'line management' occupations in contrast to the 'staff' and 'specialist' occupations included in Division 16. Also includes such occupations as officers and executives of government, corporations, and nonprofit organizations; general managers; general supervisors; and department heads and their assistants in industrial establishments. Many general administrators and managers are former scientific, professional, and administrative specialists. Care must be taken to classify occupations according to duties and requirements rather than an incumbent's education or experience. Occupations in the administration of a scientific, technical, or professional activity must be carefully scrutinized to determine whether they are concerned primarily with technical supervision or with general management or specialized administrative work. (DOT, 4th Edition, p. 107)</td></tr>
<tr></tr>
<tr><td>MANAGERS AND OFFICIALS, N.E.C.</td></tr>
</table>

Jobs held by handicapped workers:

D.O.T. JOB TITLE	MENTALLY RETARDED— Trainable	MENTALLY RETARDED— Severe & Profound	EMOTIONALLY DISTURBED	MULTIPLY HANDICAPPED	EPILEPSY	CEREBRAL PALSY	PARAPLEGIC	QUADRIPLEGIC	OTHER ORTHOPEDIC	SEVERE HEALTH	SEVERE NEUROLOGICAL
Manager, Retail Store				C				C			
Controller							C				
Administrator, Hospital										C	
Residence Supervisor						C					
Manager, Warehouse										C	
Manager, Retail Store							C				
Manager, Apartment House										C	
Management Trainee			C								

C = Competitive Employment

Other jobs in this division:

- Vice President   • Contractor   • Manager, Branch   • General Supervisor   • Director, News
- Maintenance Supervisor   • Security Officer   • Superintendent, Transportation   • Wholesaler
- Service Manager   • Real-Estate Agent   • Operations Officer   • Loan Officer
- Producer (motion picture)   • Director, Medical Facilities Section

Opening jobs in this division:

Administrative jobs may be available to handicapped persons who possess the necessary intellectual and social abilities. Communication barriers would need to be well managed. Depending upon the specific job requirements, mobility barriers may be a problem. Basic education is a necessary requirement for most jobs. Special training may augment skill development. For many jobs, the barriers caused by negative public attitudes would be amenable to the strategies suggested in the barriers section of this book.

This division includes miscellaneous occupations concerned with professional, technical, and managerial work. (DOT, 4th Edition, p. 139)

Jobs held by handicapped workers:

D.O.T. JOB TITLE	MENTALLY RETARDED— Trainable	MENTALLY RETARDED— Severe & Profound	EMOTIONALLY DISTURBED	MULTIPLY HANDICAPPED	EPILEPSY	CEREBRAL PALSY	PARAPLEGIC	QUADRIPLEGIC	OTHER ORTHOPEDIC	SEVERE HEALTH	SEVERE NEUROLOGICAL
Social Worker, Delinquency Prevention						C				C	
Social Worker, Medical						C				C	
Social Worker, Psychiatric						C				C	
Social Worker, School						C				C	
Urban Planner						C					
Dispatcher							C,S			C	
Appraiser, Real Estate										C	
Transmitter Operator										C	
Scientific Helper								C			

C = Competitive Employment; S = Sheltered Workshop

Other jobs in this division:

- Artist's Manager
- Business Manager
- Literary Agent
- Service Representative
- Radio Station Operator
- Recording Engineer
- Caseworker
- Parole Officer
- Recreation Leader
- Eligibility Worker
- Case Aide

Opening jobs in this division:

Jobs in this occupational division require high general intellectual and verbal capacities and the ability to communicate with people. Communication barriers may be overcome by various communication devices. Some jobs require considerable mobility, and thus may present a barrier to the handicapped worker. However, special devices may be used to aid mobility. Likewise, visual and hearing demands made by many of these jobs can be met with aids.

This division includes occupations concerned with making, classifying, and filing primarily verbal records. Includes activities, such as transmitting and receiving data by machines equipped with a typewriter-like keyboard, cold type typesetting, word processing, and operating machines to duplicate records, correspondence, and reports; to emboss data on metal or plastic plates for addressing and similar identification purposes; to sort, fold, insert, seal, address, and stamp mail; and to open envenopes. Occupations concerned primarily with statistical, financial, or other numerical data are found in Division 21. (DOT, 4th Edition, p. 153)

Jobs held by handicapped workers:

D.O.T. JOB TITLE	MENTALLY RETARDED— Trainable	MENTALLY RETARDED— Severe & Profound	EMOTIONALLY DISTURBED	MULTIPLY HANDICAPPED	EPILEPSY	CEREBRAL PALSY	PARAPLEGIC	QUADRIPLEGIC	OTHER ORTHOPEDIC	SEVERE HEALTH	SEVERE NEUROLOGICAL
Secretary			C				C				
Hospital Admitting Clerk										C	
Keypunch Operator			C	C		C	C			C	C
Addressing Machine Operator			C								
File Clerk I			C			C			C	C	C
Stenographer			C								
Typist			C	C	C		C			C	
Telegraphic Typewriter Operator				C							
Transcribing Machine Operator				C							
Medical Secretary										C	
Data Typist							C				
Clerk, General	C,S		C	C	C	C	C	C	C		
Clerk, Typist			C	C			C				
Mail Clerk	S		C,S	C	C	C	C			C	
Proofreader							C			C	
Sorter	C	S									
Duplicating-Machine Operator	C	C			C	C					
Offset-Duplicating-Machine Operator			C			C					
Photocopying Machine Operator	C		C								

C = Competitive Employment; S = Sheltered Workshop

Other jobs in this division:

- Shorthand Reporter
- Varitype Operator
- Credit Clerk
- Civil Service Clerk
- Traffic Checker
- Correspondence Clerk
- Title Searcher
- Meter Reader (light, heat, & power; waterworks)
- Coding Clerk
- Checker

Opening jobs in this division:

Most workers who enter these jobs are high school graduates who have received special training in typing and business methods. A satisfactory score on a typing test is usually required. Where proficiency in the operation of specific machines is required, training is usually done on the job. Many of these jobs should be open to handicapped workers who are trained, and who possess adequate mental and psychomotor abilities. Strategies for overcoming mobility, communication, and attitude barriers are relevant.

21

COMPUTING AND ACCOUNT-RECORDING

This division includes occupations concerned with systematizing information about transactions and activities into accounts and quantitative records, and paying and receiving money. It includes such activities as keeping and verifying records of business or financial transactions; receiving and disbursing money in banks or other establishments; operating electronic and electromechanical data-processing machines and equipment; computing and verifying amounts due for goods and services; preparing payrolls, timekeeping records, and duty rosters; posting primary financial or statistical data to accounting records; and computing costs of production in relation to other factors to determine profit and loss. Activities concerned with computing amounts of materials, equipment, and labor to determine production costs; and activities concerned with electronic and electromechanical machines and equipment to coordinate, schedule, or monitor production processes are found in Division 22. (DOT, 4th Edition, p. 164)

Jobs held by handicapped workers:

D.O.T. JOB TITLE	MENTALLY RETARDED—Trainable	MENTALLY RETARDED—Severe & Profound	EMOTIONALLY DISTURBED	MULTIPLY HANDICAPPED	EPILEPSY	CEREBRAL PALSY	PARAPLEGIC	QUADRIPLEGIC	OTHER ORTHOPEDIC	SEVERE HEALTH	SEVERE NEUROLOGICAL
Cashier I			C			C	C				
Computer Operator						C					
Insurance Clerk I							C				
Merchandise Distributor				C							
Bookeeper I				C	C		C	C			
Bookkeeping-Machine Operator									C		
Administrative Clerk							C		C	C	
Billing Typist				C							
Calculating Machine Operator			C								
Accounting Clerk						C	C		C		
Cashier II			C	C	C	C	C,S			C	

C = Competitive Employment; S = Sheltered Workshop

Other jobs in this division:

- Teller - Toll Collector - Ticket Seller - Food Checker - Rater (insurance) - Payroll Clerk
- Collection Clerk - Probate Clerk - Proof-Machine Operator - Statement Clerk

Opening jobs in this division:

Many jobs in this division should be open to handicapped workers who have arithmetical and clerical ability and a general knowledge of the work and the equipment involved. Special training may augment skill development. Persons without the use of arms and hands will usually be excluded from these jobs unless the jobs have been redesigned or special equipment has been adapted to their requirements. Communication barriers may be circumvented with communication devices. The handicapped worker's demonstrated competency should be effective in overcoming attitude barriers.

This division includes occupations concerned with compiling and maintaining production records, expediting flow of work and materials, and receiving, storing, shipping, issuing, requisitioning, and accounting for materials and goods. (DOT, 4th Edition, p. 179)

Jobs held by handicapped workers:

D.O.T. JOB TITLE	MENTALLY RETARDED—Trainable	MENTALLY RETARDED—Severe & Profound	EMOTIONALLY DISTURBED	MULTIPLY HANDICAPPED	EPILEPSY	CEREBRAL PALSY	PARAPLEGIC	QUADRIPLEGIC	OTHER ORTHOPEDIC	SEVERE HEALTH	SEVERE NEUROLOGICAL
Shipping and Receiving Clerk				C	C						C
Material Clerk								C			
Stock Clerk	C		C	C	C		C			C	
Storekeeper										C	
Tool Crib Attendant									C		
Estimator, Printing							C				
Inventory Clerk								C		C	
Sales Correspondent								C			
Aircraft Shipping Checker	C										
Laboratory Clerk			C				C		C	C	
Mailer	C										
Route-Delivery Clerk										C	

C = Competitive Employment

Other jobs in this division:

- Supervisor, Production Clerk
- Service Clerk
- Job Tracer
- Laundry Clerk
- Cargo Checker
- Parcel-Post Clerk
- Meat Clerk
- Garment Sorter

Opening jobs in this division:

These jobs appear to be promising for severely handicapped persons who have the ability to obtain pertinent information by reading (or some other method), to do required arithmetical computations, etc. A mobility handicap would be a barrier in some jobs but not in others. Communication handicaps are not critical for many jobs and could be managed by communication devices. On-the-job training would be required and, in many cases, employers may require a high school diploma or its equivalent, with successful completion of commercial courses and demonstrated familiarity with elementary clerical skills.

23

INFORMATION
AND MESSAGE
DISTRIBUTION

This division includes occupations concerned with the distribution of information and messages by direct personal or telephone contact, involving such activities as delivering mail, relaying messages by telephone or telegraph equipment, arranging travel accommodations, and directing visitors at reception points. (DOT, 4th Edition, p. 190)

Jobs held by handicapped workers:

D.O.T. JOB TITLE	MENTALLY RETARDED—Trainable	MENTALLY RETARDED—Severe & Profound	EMOTIONALLY DISTURBED	MULTIPLY HANDICAPPED	EPILEPSY	CEREBRAL PALSY	PARAPLEGIC	QUADRIPLEGIC	OTHER ORTHOPEDIC	SEVERE HEALTH	SEVERE NEUROLOGICAL
Telephone Operator, Chief										C	
Hotel Clerk			C						C		
Reservation Clerk			C							C	
Information Clerk										C	
Receptionist			C	C		C	C	C		C	
Mail Carrier						C					
Dispatcher, Maintenance Service				C						C	
Central Office Operator							C				
Telephone Answering Service Operator										C	
Telephone Operator	S		C	C		C	C,S	C		C	
Deliverer, Outside	C		C	C		C				C	

C = Competitive Employment; S = Sheltered Workshop

Other jobs in this division:

- Messenger, Bank
- Appointment Clerk
- Manager, Reservations
- Ticket Agent
- Office Helper
- Travel Clerk
- Telegrapher
- Switchboard Operator, Police District

Opening jobs in this division:

The ability to communicate with strangers is required in practically all of these jobs. Thus, the person who cannot speak or hear well faces a substantial barrier. Rarely do these jobs require heavy lifting, and what equipment must be used, such as telephones, can be adapted for use by people with almost any physical handicap. Mobility barriers should be less on these jobs than on those in most other divisions. Some attitudinal barriers may be expected, particularly by those with poor speech, awkward movements, or cosmetic abnormalities.

24

MISCELLANEOUS
CLERICAL

This division includes miscellaneous occupations concerned with clerical work. (DOT, 4th Edition, p. 195)

Jobs held by handicapped workers:

D.O.T. JOB TITLE	MENTALLY RETARDED—Trainable	MENTALLY RETARDED—Severe & Profound	EMOTIONALLY DISTURBED	MULTIPLY HANDICAPPED	EPILEPSY	CEREBRAL PALSY	PARAPLEGIC	QUADRIPLEGIC	OTHER ORTHOPEDIC	SEVERE HEALTH	SEVERE NEUROLOGICAL
Dispatcher, Motor Vehicle							C				
Classified Ad Clerk I			C								
Page			C		C					C	
Order Clerk		C				C		C			
Collection Clerk											C
Procurement Clerk										C	

C = Competitive Employment

77

Other jobs in this division:

- Claims Adjuster
- Claims Examiner
- Investigator
- Loan Interviewer
- Repossessor
- Skip Tracer
- Court Clerk
- Post-Office Clerk
- Medical-Record Clerk
- Teacher Aide II

Opening jobs in this division:

Barriers and methods for overcoming them are similar to those discussed for Occupational Divisions 20 to 23, above.

25
SALES OCCUPATIONS, SERVICES

This division includes occupations concerned with selling real estate, insurance, securities, and other business, financial, and consumer services. (DOT, 4th Edition, p. 204)

Jobs held by handicapped workers:

D.O.T. JOB TITLE	MENTALLY RETARDED— Trainable	MENTALLY RETARDED— Severe & Profound	EMOTIONALLY DISTURBED	MULTIPLY HANDICAPPED	EPILEPSY	CEREBRAL PALSY	PARAPLEGIC	QUADRIPLEGIC	OTHER ORTHOPEDIC	SEVERE HEALTH	SEVERE NEUROLOGICAL
Sales Representative, Advertising								C			

C = Competitive Employment

Other jobs in this division:

- Sales Agent, Business Services
- Sales Agent, Securities
- Sales Representative, Telephone Service
- Sales Representative, Signs and Displays
- Communications Consultant
- Group-Sales Representative

Opening jobs in this division:

The ability to communicate is a prerequisite for most of these jobs. Public attitudes and mobility are barriers that require careful management. Since these jobs require direct contact with people, and success depends largely upon public acceptance, careful consideration must be given to presenting a pleasing public image. One advantage in many of these jobs, as distinct from some others in which public attitudes may be a barrier, is that business relationships are long-term. Thus, once an initially skeptical client is won over, repeat business may be expected, and attitudinal barriers will not have to be overcome anew for each business contact. Mobility requirements vary considerably. Thus, even though some positions may present significant barriers, it should be possible to find a job within the capabilities of most orthopedically handicapped people.

26
SALES OCCUPATIONS, CONSUMABLE COMMODITIES

This division includes occupations concerned with selling consumable commodities, such as farm produce and livestock, foodstuffs, textiles, apparel, fuels and petroleum products, chemicals, and drug preparations, when knowledge of the commodities sold is required. (DOT, 4th Edition, p. 207)

Jobs held by handicapped workers:

D.O.T. JOB TITLE	MENTALLY RETARDED— Trainable	MENTALLY RETARDED— Severe & Profound	EMOTIONALLY DISTURBED	MULTIPLY HANDICAPPED	EPILEPSY	CEREBRAL PALSY	PARAPLEGIC	QUADRIPLEGIC	OTHER ORTHOPEDIC	SEVERE HEALTH	SEVERE NEUROLOGICAL
Sales Representative, Food Products			C								

C = Competitive Employment

Other jobs in this division:

- Sales Representative, Footwear
- Sales Representative, Women's and Girls' Apparel
- Salesperson, Cosmetics and Toiletries
- Salesperson, Men's Furnishings

Opening jobs in this division:

The ability to communicate is a prerequisite for most of these jobs. Public attitudes and mobility are barriers that require careful management. Since these jobs require direct contact with people, and success depends largely upon public acceptance, careful consideration must be given to presenting a pleasing public image. Many jobs in this division involve repeated sales contacts. Thus, initial reluctance to deal with a handicapped person need not be overcome for each transaction.

27

SALES OCCUPATIONS,
COMMODITIES, N.E.C.

This division includes occupations concerned with selling commodities, not included in Division 26, when knowledge of the commodities sold is required. (DOT, 4th Edition, p. 209)

Jobs held by handicapped workers:

D.O.T. JOB TITLE	MENTALLY RETARDED—Trainable	MENTALLY RETARDED—Severe & Profound	EMOTIONALLY DISTURBED	MULTIPLY HANDICAPPED	EPILEPSY	CEREBRAL PALSY	PARAPLEGIC	QUADRIPLEGIC	OTHER ORTHOPEDIC	SEVERE HEALTH	SEVERE NEUROLOGICAL
Sales Representative, Dental and Medical Equipment and Supplies										C	
Sales Representative, Farm and Garden Equipment and Supplies								C			
Sales Representative, Office Machines			C								
Salesperson, Automobiles								C		C	
Sales Representative, Jewelry										C	
Sales Representative, Novelties											C
Sales Representative, General Merchandise			C								
Salesperson, Parts				C							

C = Competitive Employment

Other jobs in this division:

- Salesperson, Florist Supplies
- Salesperson, Sewing Machines
- Salesperson, Furniture
- Salesperson, Stereo Equipment
- Salesperson, Automobile Accessories
- Salesperson, Trailers and Motor Homes
- Sales Representatives, Computer and EDP Systems
- Salesperson, Surgical Appliances

Opening jobs in this division:

The ability to interact with strangers is required in practially all of these jobs. Thus, the person who cannot speak or hear well, who has awkward movements or cosmetic abnormalities may face serious attitudinal barriers. Another problem that will arise is that persons with certain physical handicaps will not be able to demonstrate unmodified equipment of the types sold in many of these occupations. The keys to overcoming these barriers are knowing about the items sold to reassure the customer about the competence of the salesperson and making arrangements for satisfactory demonstration. The latter can be achieved by the salesperson operating modified equipment, having another person make those demonstrations beyond the capability of the salesperson, or having the salesperson instruct the customer in the operation of the equipment where this is practical.

<table>
<tr><td>29</td><td rowspan="2">This division includes occupations concerned with sales transactions, except those of sales representatives and salespersons which are included in Divisions 25, 26, and 27, and occupations closely related to sales transactions, even though they do not involve actual participation in such transactions. (DOT, 4th Edition, p. 215)</td></tr>
<tr><td>MISCELLANEOUS SALES</td></tr>
</table>

Jobs held by handicapped workers:

D.O.T. JOB TITLE	MENTALLY RETARDED— Trainable	MENTALLY RETARDED— Severe & Profound	EMOTIONALLY DISTURBED	MULTIPLY HANDICAPPED	EPILEPSY	CEREBRAL PALSY	PARAPLEGIC	QUADRIPLEGIC	OTHER ORTHOPEDIC	SEVERE HEALTH	SEVERE NEUROLOGICAL
Sales Representative, Door-to-Door								C			
Telephone Solicitor			C	C	C	C	C,S*	C	C	C	C
Sales Clerk			C	C					C	C	
Vendor							C				
Newspaper Carrier									C		
Sandwich-Board Carrier	C,S	S									

C = Competitive Employment; S = Sheltered Workshop
*Also homebound

Other jobs in this division:

- Cigarette Vendor
- Newspaper-Delivery Driver
- Lunch-Truck Driver
- Fund Raiser
- Auctioneer
- Model
- Decorator
- Gift Wrapper
- Optician Dispensing II

Opening jobs in this division:

The ability to communicate is a prerequisite for most of these jobs. Public attitudes and mobility are barriers that require careful management. Since these jobs require direct contact with people, and success depends largely upon public acceptance, careful consideration must be given to presenting a pleasing public image. Many of these jobs require considerable mobility; however, numerous persons who have a variety of handicapping conditions presently hold jobs in this group, indicating that some of the jobs (e.g., telephone solicitor) appear to have many advantages for the handicapped.

This division includes occupations concerned with tasks in and around a private household. (DOT, 4th Edition, p. 223)

Jobs held by handicapped workers:

D.O.T. JOB TITLE	MENTALLY RETARDED—Trainable	MENTALLY RETARDED—Severe & Profound	EMOTIONALLY DISTURBED	MULTIPLY HANDICAPPED	EPILEPSY	CEREBRAL PALSY	PARAPLEGIC	QUADRIPLEGIC	OTHER ORTHOPEDIC	SEVERE HEALTH	SEVERE NEUROLOGICAL
Cook (domestic service)									C		
House Worker, General	C,S	C,S	C	C			C				
Personal Attendant						C					
Child Monitor	C			C							
Companion			C	C							
Foster Parent			C								

C = Competitive Employment; S = Sheltered Workshop

Other jobs in this division:

● Caretaker   ● Yard Worker   ● Day Worker

Opening jobs in this division:

Many severely handicapped workers are presently employed in the jobs in this occupational division. Barriers that may preclude employment are severe communication or mobility handicaps.

FOOD AND BEVERAGE
PREPARATION AND
SERVICE OCCUPATIONS

This division includes occupations concerned with preparing food and beverages and serving them to patrons of such establishments as hotels, clubs, restaurants, and cocktail lounges. (DOT, 4th Edition, p. 224)

Jobs held by handicapped workers:

D.O.T. JOB TITLE	MENTALLY RETARDED— Trainable	MENTALLY RETARDED— Severe & Profound	EMOTIONALLY DISTURBED	MULTIPLY HANDICAPPED	EPILEPSY	CEREBRAL PALSY	PARAPLEGIC	QUADRIPLEGIC	OTHER ORTHOPEDIC	SEVERE HEALTH	SEVERE NEUROLOGICAL
Steward/Stewardess, Banquet										C	
Cook (unspecified)			C							C	
Cook (hotel and restaurant)										C	
Cook, Short Order I	C,S		C	C	C						
Dining Room Attendant	C,S	S	C	C	C	C					
Steamtable Worker	C										
Counter Attendant, Cafeteria	C,S	S			C						
Salad Counter Attendant	C,S	S									
Canteen Operator					C						
Waiter/Waitress	C,S		C	C						C	
Bartender			C								
Fountain Server	C,S	S			C						
Salad Maker					C	C					
Dishwasher, Hand	C		C								
Kitchen Helper	C,S	C,S		C	C	C	C		C		C

C = Competitive Employment; S = Sheltered Workshop

Other jobs in this division:

- Host/Hostess, Restaurant   • Car Hop   • Baker, Head   • Carver   • Butcher, Meat (hotel & rest.)
- Sandwich Maker   • Cook Helper   • Caterer Helper

Opening jobs in this division:

Many severely handicapped persons with a variety of handicapping conditions are presently holding jobs in this occupational division. They are employed both in sheltered workshops and in competitive employment. Formal education is not a requirement for obtaining employment, although many employers prefer that employees have a high school education. Special courses may be given by hotel and restaurant associations or by individual establishments. Job redesign or simplification may be appropriate for some handicapping conditions. Persons with severe communication, mobility, or cosmetic handicaps may face substantial barriers in some of these jobs.

This division includes occupations concerned with providing accommodations to guests in boarding houses or lodging houses. (DOT, 4th Edition, p. 231)

Jobs held by handicapped workers:

D.O.T. JOB TITLE	MENTALLY RETARDED— Trainable	MENTALLY RETARDED— Severe & Profound	EMOTIONALLY DISTURBED	MULTIPLY HANDICAPPED	EPILEPSY	CEREBRAL PALSY	PARAPLEGIC	QUADRIPLEGIC	OTHER ORTHOPEDIC	SEVERE HEALTH	SEVERE NEUROLOGICAL
Bellhop	C										
Housecleaner					C					C	
Cleaner, Housekeeping				C	C,S	C				C	
Cleaner, Hospital			C								

C = Competitive Employment; S = Sheltered Workshop

Other jobs in this division:

● Manager, Boarding House   ● Porter, Baggage   ● Doorkeeper   ● Attendant, Campground

Opening jobs in this division:

The most important factor for obtaining jobs in this occupational division is the ability of the applicant to meet the strength requirements which range from light to very heavy. Because many nonhandicapped applicants can qualify for these jobs, personal characteristics such as reliability, honesty, and industry will play a significant role in job retention for the handicapped. Workers with orthopedic handicaps will be excluded from many of these jobs. Communication and learning handicaps need not be serious barriers if appropriate strategies are used to manage them. Since many severely handicapped persons are presently working at many of these jobs, attitudes would not seem to be a major barrier.

33

BARBERING,
COSMETOLOGY, AND
RELATED SERVICE
OCCUPATIONS

This division includes occupations concerned with rendering beauty and/or related treatments to individuals. (DOT, 4th Edition, p. 233)

Jobs held by handicapped workers:

D.O.T. JOB TITLE	MENTALLY RETARDED—Trainable	MENTALLY RETARDED—Severe & Profound	EMOTIONALLY DISTURBED	MULTIPLY HANDICAPPED	EPILEPSY	CEREBRAL PALSY	PARAPLEGIC	QUADRIPLEGIC	OTHER ORTHOPEDIC	SEVERE HEALTH	SEVERE NEUROLOGICAL
Barber				C			C				C
Mortuary Beautician				C							
Supply Clerk										C	

C = Competitive Employment

Other jobs in this division:

- Make-Up Artist
- Masseur/Masseuse
- Embalmer
- Electrologist
- Tattoo Artist
- Manager, Health Club
- Scalp-Treatment Operator

Opening jobs in this division:

Major barriers for handicapped workers include the inability to use the arms and hands, negative public attitudes, and, to some extent, the inability to communicate. Orthopedically handicapped persons who are able to use their arms and hands may find special mobility devices useful. Special training may be required to augment skills or cosmetic appearance. Licensing requirements may be a barrier to those persons who lack formal training.

34

AMUSEMENT AND
RECREATION
SERVICE
OCCUPATIONS

This division includes occupations concerned with amusement and recreation services. (DOT, 4th Edition, p. 235)

Jobs held by handicapped workers:

D.O.T. JOB TITLE	MENTALLY RETARDED— Trainable	MENTALLY RETARDED— Severe & Profound	EMOTIONALLY DISTURBED	MULTIPLY HANDICAPPED	EPILEPSY	CEREBRAL PALSY	PARAPLEGIC	QUADRIPLEGIC	OTHER ORTHOPEDIC	SEVERE HEALTH	SEVERE NEUROLOGICAL
Recreation-Facility Attendant							C				

C = Competitive Employment

Other jobs in this division:

- Game Attendant
- Barker
- Gambling Dealer
- Ticket Taker
- Usher
- Costumer
- Caddie
- Desk Clerk, Bowling Floor

Opening jobs in this division:

Most jobs in this division require interaction with the public (one exception is costumer). Those who have trouble communicating will have serious problems, and techniques for communication that help the person perform in a "normal" fashion, such as speech therapy, may be effective. Physical requirements vary greatly, and the careful selection of a job slot combined with aids and architectural changes is the key to success.

35

MISCELLANEOUS
PERSONAL SERVICE
OCCUPATIONS

This division includes occupations concerned with those duties performed by stewards and hostesses, not elsewhere classified, and attendants, guides, and the like. (DOT, 4th Edition, p. 238)

Jobs held by handicapped workers:

D.O.T. JOB TITLE	MENTALLY RETARDED— Trainable	MENTALLY RETARDED— Severe & Profound	EMOTIONALLY DISTURBED	MULTIPLY HANDICAPPED	EPILEPSY	CEREBRAL PALSY	PARAPLEGIC	QUADRIPLEGIC	OTHER ORTHOPEDIC	SEVERE HEALTH	SEVERE NEUROLOGICAL
Occupational Therapy Aide			C	C				C		C	
Escort										C	
Porter			C								
Child-Care Attendant, School	C										
Nurse Aide	C		C	C	C	C	C	C		C	C
Orderly	C	C	C	C	C					C	
Physical Therapy Aide				C						C	
Food-Service Worker, Hospital	C		C			C	C				
Nursery School Attendant			C							C	
Morgue Attendant			C				C				

C = Competitive Employment

Other jobs in this division:

- Director, Social
- Ambulance Attendant
- Airplane-Flight Attendant
- Restroom Attendant
- Guide, Travel
- Chauffeur, Funeral Car
- Nurse, Practical

Opening jobs in this division:

Job demands vary so greatly in this division that it is difficult to identify barriers of special significance to the group as a whole.

36

APPAREL AND
FURNISHINGS
SERVICE
OCCUPATIONS

This division includes occupations concerned with improving the appearance of and repairing clothing, furnishings, and accessories. (DOT, 4th Edition, p. 243)

Jobs held by handicapped workers:

D.O.T. JOB TITLE	MENTALLY RETARDED—Trainable	MENTALLY RETARDED—Severe & Profound	EMOTIONALLY DISTURBED	MULTIPLY HANDICAPPED	EPILEPSY	CEREBRAL PALSY	PARAPLEGIC	QUADRIPLEGIC	OTHER ORTHOPEDIC	SEVERE HEALTH	SEVERE NEUROLOGICAL
Supervisor, Dry Cleaning								C			
Shoe Repairer				C		C					
Presser, Machine	C		C	C							
Shoe-Repairer Helper				C		C					
Laundry Operator										C	
Dry Cleaner Helper				C							
Laundry Worker I			C			C					
Laundry Laborer			C,S	C							
Washer, Hand	C,S	C	C								
Laundry Worker III	C			C							

C = Competitive Employment; S = Sheltered Workshop

Other jobs in this division:

- Spotter
- Fur Cleaner
- Leather Cleaner
- Silk Finisher
- Blocker
- Dyer
- Manager, Laundromat
- Rug Cleaner, Hand

Opening jobs in this division:

A large number of jobs in this occupational division are already available to severely handicapped workers with a variety of handicapping conditions. Not only are these jobs available in competitive employment, but many are available in sheltered workshops that have been specifically designed to accommodate severely handicapped persons. Special training is often used to augment skills, and significant progress has recently been made with handicapped persons such as the severely mentally retarded. Severe orthopedic handicaps, which limit the manipulation of objects and tools, may prohibit work in certain of these jobs. Communication handicaps are probably not critical, providing they can be circumvented by sign language and communication devices.

This division includes occupations concerned with protecting the public against crime, fire, accidents, and acts of war. (DOT, 4th Edition, p. 251)

Jobs held by handicapped workers:

D.O.T. JOB TITLE	MENTALLY RETARDED—Trainable	MENTALLY RETARDED—Severe & Profound	EMOTIONALLY DISTURBED	MULTIPLY HANDICAPPED	EPILEPSY	CEREBRAL PALSY	PARAPLEGIC	QUADRIPLEGIC	OTHER ORTHOPEDIC	SEVERE HEALTH	SEVERE NEUROLOGICAL
Dectective					C*						
Guard, Security	C		C		C	C			C	C	
Protective Officer							C				

C = Competitive Employment; *Trainee in Competitive Employment

Other jobs in this division:

- Special Agent
- Airline Security Representative
- Bodyguard
- School Bus Monitor
- Fire Fighter
- Fingerprint Classifier
- Desk Officer
- Lifeguard
- Dog Catcher

Opening jobs in this division:

Because this work involves the protection of life and property, workers are usually required to undergo rigid training and to pass difficult tests before they qualify for jobs. Special training for qualified criminal investigation work may be helpful to selected handicapped workers, as such skills are in demand. Mobility and communication handicaps may prohibit work in some of these jobs unless adequate adaptive devices can be obtained and utilized. Also, anyone lacking the intellitual ability and emotional stability needed to make sensible decisions in difficult circumstances would be excluded from many of these jobs.

This division includes occupations concerned with the cleaning and upkeep of building interiors and the conveying of passengers and freight by elevator. (DOT, 4th Edition, p. 264)

Jobs held by handicapped workers:

D.O.T. JOB TITLE	MENTALLY RETARDED— Trainable	MENTALLY RETARDED— Severe & Profound	EMOTIONALLY DISTURBED	MULTIPLY HANDICAPPED	EPILEPSY	CEREBRAL PALSY	PARAPLEGIC	QUADRIPLEGIC	OTHER ORTHOPEDIC	SEVERE HEALTH	SEVERE NEUROLOGICAL
Janitor			C	C		C	C		C	C	
Cleaner, Laboratory Equipment			C								
Cleaner, Commercial or Institutional	C,S	C,S	C	C	C,S	C,S				C	C
Cleaner, Window	C										

C = Competitive Employment; S = Sheltered Workshop

Other jobs in this division:

- Fumigator
- Exterminator Helper, Termite
- Elevator Operator
- Sweeper-Cleaner, Industrial
- Exterminator
- Cleaner, Wall
- Waxer, Floor

Opening jobs in this division:

One of the most important hiring factors for jobs in this division is the ability of the applicant to meet the strength requirements. Because many nonhandicapped applicants can qualify for these jobs, personal characteristics such as reliability, honesty, and industry will play a significant role in job retention for the handicapped. Workers with orthopedic handicaps will be excluded from many of these jobs. Communication and learning handicaps need not be serious barriers on many jobs if appropriate strategies are used to manage them. Since many severely handicapped persons are presently working in jobs in this division, attitudes would not seem to be a major barrier.

<table>
<tr><td>40</td></tr>
<tr><td>PLANT FARMING OCCUPATIONS</td></tr>
</table>

This division includes occupations concerned with tilling soil; propagating, cultivating, and harvesting plant life; gathering products of plant life; and caring for parks, gardens, and grounds. Service occupations performed in support of these activities are also included. (DOT, 4th Edition, p. 267)

Jobs held by handicapped workers:

D.O.T. JOB TITLE	MENTALLY RETARDED— Trainable	MENTALLY RETARDED— Severe & Profound	EMOTIONALLY DISTURBED	MULTIPLY HANDICAPPED	EPILEPSY	CEREBRAL PALSY	PARAPLEGIC	QUADRIPLEGIC	OTHER ORTHOPEDIC	SEVERE HEALTH	SEVERE NEUROLOGICAL
Groundskeeper, Industrial-Commericial	C,S	S	C	C							
Farm Worker, Vegetable II	C	C,S	C								

C = Competitive Employment; S = Sheltered Workshop

Other jobs in this division:

- Harvest Worker, Vegetable
- Farmworker, Fruit I
- Farmer, Field Crop
- Horticultural Worker I
- Flower Picker
- Cemetery Worker
- Landscape Gardener
- Tree Surgeon
- Tree Trimmer
- Irrigator, Head

Opening jobs in this division:

Intellectual and physical demands vary substantially from job to job in this division. Thus, many handicapped workers will be able to identify jobs in which they might succeed. For example, the retarded can do cultivation and harvesting tasks, and the orthopedically handicapped can perform management fuctions on large farms where field supervision is the responsibility of others. Attitudinal barriers may be substantial as many workers are likely to feel that supervisory personnel should have "come through the ranks" when this will clearly not be the case for most orthopedically handicapped persons. Removal of work environment barriers will probably be either routine, as in the case of supervisory offices and greenhouses used for propagation, or insurmountable, as in the case of field occupations.

41
ANIMAL FARMING OCCUPATIONS

This division includes occupations concerned with breeding, raising, maintaining, gathering, and caring for land animals, collecting their products, and providing services in support of these activities. Occupations concerned with breeding and caring for aquatic animals are included in Division 44. (DOT, 4th Edition, p. 275)

Jobs held by handicapped workers:

D.O.T. JOB TITLE	MENTALLY RETARDED— Trainable	MENTALLY RETARDED— Severe & Profound	EMOTIONALLY DISTURBED	MULTIPLY HANDICAPPED	EPILEPSY	CEREBRAL PALSY	PARAPLEGIC	QUADRIPLEGIC	OTHER ORTHOPEDIC	SEVERE HEALTH	SEVERE NEUROLOGICAL
Dog Bather	C										
Kennel Attendant						C			C		

C = Competitive Employment

Other jobs in this division:

- Animal Breeder
- Animal Caretaker
- Milker, Machine
- Sheep Herder
- Poultry Farmer
- Animal Keeper
- Horseshoer
- Dog Groomer
- Horse Trainer

Opening jobs in this division:

See division 40, Plant Farming Occupations for intellectual and physical demands that also apply to jobs in this division.

51

ORE REFINING
AND FOUNDRY
OCCUPATIONS

This division includes occupations concerned with reducing, smelting, refining, or alloying metalliferous extracted ore, ore concentrate, pig, or scrap; and casting ingots, shapes for further processing, and finished metal products in a foundry. (DOT, 4th Edition, p. 298)

Jobs held by handicapped workers:

D.O.T. JOB TITLE	MENTALLY RETARDED— Trainable	MENTALLY RETARDED— Severe & Profound	EMOTIONALLY DISTURBED	MULTIPLY HANDICAPPED	EPILEPSY	CEREBRAL PALSY	PARAPLEGIC	QUADRIPLEGIC	OTHER ORTHOPEDIC	SEVERE HEALTH	SEVERE NEUROLOGICAL
Foundry Worker, General			C	C							

C = Competitive Employment

Other jobs in this division:

- Dust Mixer
- Kettle Tender
- Supervisor, Blast Furnace
- Furnace Operator
- Metal Control Worker
- Die-Casting-Machine Setter
- Mold Worker
- Ladle Pourer
- Lime Mixer Tender
- Grinding-Mill Operator
- Plaster Molder

Opening jobs in this division:

Practically every job in this division requires extensive physical activity. Generally, modifications to allow the severely physically handicapped to do these jobs would be difficult, if not impossible. The greatest promise for the physically handicapped would come from increased automation. This, however, would probably be done by industry in the course of modernization and would be prohibitively expensive to do for a given individual. Some jobs may be open to the retarded who can meet the strength requirements. Careful job selection and training should be undertaken to assure that workers are able to deal with potentially dangerous situations that may arise in many of these jobs.

52

PROCESSING OF FOOD,
TOBACCO, AND
RELATED PRODUCTS

This division includes occupations concerned with preparing food, tobacco, and related products for commercial use. Includes manufacturing phases after harvesting and prior to marketing. Such activities as slaughtering livestock, blending cheeses, fermenting alcohol, and smoking hams are included in this division. Marking and packaging occupations are included here when they occur at the end of a production process. (DOT, 4th Edition, p. 314)

Jobs held by handicapped workers:

D.O.T. JOB TITLE	MENTALLY RETARDED— Trainable	MENTALLY RETARDED— Severe & Profound	EMOTIONALLY DISTURBED	MULTIPLY HANDICAPPED	EPILEPSY	CEREBRAL PALSY	PARAPLEGIC	QUADRIPLEGIC	OTHER ORTHOPEDIC	SEVERE HEALTH	SEVERE NEUROLOGICAL
Baker Helper	C,S	S									
Container Washer, Machine	C										
Cook Helper	C,S	S	C	C						C	

C = Competitive Employment; S = Sheltered Workshop

Other jobs in this division:

- Blending Supervisor
- Dry-Starch Operator
- Dough-Mixer Operator
- Batter Mixer
- Fruit-Press Operator
- Spice Cleaner
- Liquor Blender
- Pickler
- Cheesemaker
- Tobacco-Drier Operator
- Cake Decorator
- Fish Cleaner
- Hide Inspector

Opening jobs in this division:

Jobs in this division vary greatly in the demands placed on the worker. Thus, each of the strategies for overcoming barriers is likely to be required in accommodating those seeking jobs in this division.

<table>
<tr><td>55</td></tr>
<tr><td>PROCESSING OF CHEMICALS, PLASTICS, SYNTHETICS, RUBBER, PAINT, AND RELATED PRODUCTS</td></tr>
</table>

This division includes occupations concerned with manufacturing basic chemicals, such as acids, alkalies, salts, and organic chemicals; chemical products to be used in further manufacture, such as synthetic fibers, synthetic rubber, dry colors, and pigments; finished chemical products to be used as materials in other industries, such as paints, fertilizers, and explosives; plastics powders, granules, pellets, liquids; plastics sheets, blocks, rods, tubes, and laminations; and rubber-stock shapes and objects from natural, synthetic, or reclaimed rubber. (DOT, 4th Edition, p. 384)

Jobs held by handicapped workers:

D.O.T. JOB TITLE	MENTALLY RETARDED— Trainable	MENTALLY RETARDED— Severe & Profound	EMOTIONALLY DISTURBED	MULTIPLY HANDICAPPED	EPILEPSY	CEREBRAL PALSY	PARAPLEGIC	QUADRIPLEGIC	OTHER ORTHOPEDIC	SEVERE HEALTH	SEVERE NEUROLOGICAL
Paint Mixer, Machine			C			C				C	

C = Competitive Employment

Other jobs in this division:

- Color Matcher
- Color Maker
- Chemical Mixer
- Cement Mixer
- Purification Operator
- Screen Operator
- Distiller
- Varnish Maker
- Heat Welder, Plastics
- Pulverizer-Mill Operator
- Sand-Mill Grinder
- Casting-Room Operator

Opening jobs in this division:

Persons who have had some experience working with machines in a school or work environment are frequently preferred for these jobs. On-the-job training is the most common method by which workers attain competence. Physical and mobility requirements for these jobs will vary greatly depending upon the machine to be operated and the nature of the controls. Controls may be modified for the benefit of the individual handicapped worker. Communication barriers may not be a serious obstacle once skill is obtained. Special training prior to on-the-job training may be advisable to ensure the handicapped worker's confidence and to increase his or her experience. Intellectual demands vary greatly as a function of the degree of supervisory responsibility and the type of equipment operated.

PROCESSING OF
STONE, CLAY,
GLASS, AND
RELATED PRODUCTS

This division includes occupations concerned with preparing for market raw materials, such as stone, clay, glass, and sand. Includes abrasive, asbestos, and miscellaneous nonmetallic mineral materials; forming such materials and adjuncts in their plastic or moldable states into stock shapes, parts, and other products; and impregnating, coating, heat treating, and thermal finishing such materials and formed products. Includes fiberglass. (DOT, 4th Edition, p. 438)

Jobs held by handicapped workers:

D.O.T. JOB TITLE	MENTALLY RETARDED—Trainable	MENTALLY RETARDED—Severe & Profound	EMOTIONALLY DISTURBED	MULTIPLY HANDICAPPED	EPILEPSY	CEREBRAL PALSY	PARAPLEGIC	QUADRIPLEGIC	OTHER ORTHOPEDIC	SEVERE HEALTH	SEVERE NEUROLOGICAL
Round-Up-Ring Hand									C		

C = Competitive Employment

Other jobs in this division:

- Dry-Kiln Operator
- Glazing-Machine Operator
- File Sorter
- Silvering Applicator (mirror)
- Fiberglass-Machine Operator
- Press Operator
- Caster
- Molder Helper
- Glass Inspector

Opening jobs in this division:

Applicants for jobs in this division must be able to handle light to very heavy loads. Many nonhandicapped people can qualify for these jobs, so personal traits such as reliability, honesty, and industry will be important considerations. Workers with orthopedic handicaps will not be able to handle many of these jobs. Communication handicaps need not be serious barriers if appropriate strategies are used to manage them. Additudinal problems, if any, should decline as a handicapped worker demonstrates competence.

This division includes occupations, not elsewhere classified, concerned with processing materials and products. (DOT, 4th Edition, p. 478)

Jobs held by handicapped workers:

D.O.T. JOB TITLE	MENTALLY RETARDED— Trainable	MENTALLY RETARDED— Severe & Profound	EMOTIONALLY DISTURBED	MULTIPLY HANDICAPPED	EPILEPSY	CEREBRAL PALSY	PARAPLEGIC	QUADRIPLEGIC	OTHER ORTHOPEDIC	SEVERE HEALTH	SEVERE NEUROLOGICAL
Printed Circuit Technician			C				C				

C = Competitive Employment

Other jobs in this division:

- Supervisor, Electronics Processing
- Operator, Automated Process
- Diamond Blender
- Jewelry Coater
- Lacquerer
- Spray-Machine Tender
- Lead Handler

Opening jobs in this division:

Job requirements in this division vary so substantially that it is impossible to identify the most likely barriers.

<table>
<tr>
<td rowspan="2">60</td>
<td>This division includes occupations concerned with shaping metal parts or products through the use of cutting tools, with or without removing excess material from stock or objects, primarily by such means as cutting, boring, milling, broaching, turning, sawing, abrading, and planing. Includes laying out, job setting, repairing, maintaining, calibrating, fitting, and assembling. The machining of non-metallic materials is also included when the methods and machine tools commonly applied to the machining of metal are used. Occupations primarily concerned with the machining of clay, glass, and related materials are included in Division 67. (DOT, 4th Edition, p. 487)</td>
</tr>
</table>

METAL MACHINING OCCUPATIONS

Jobs held by handicapped workers:

D.O.T. JOB TITLE	MENTALLY RETARDED— Trainable	MENTALLY RETARDED— Severe & Profound	EMOTIONALLY DISTURBED	MULTIPLY HANDICAPPED	EPILEPSY	CEREBRAL PALSY	PARAPLEGIC	QUADRIPLEGIC	OTHER ORTHOPEDIC	SEVERE HEALTH	SEVERE NEUROLOGICAL
Machinist, Apprentice			C								
Machine Set-up Operator				C							
Turret-Lathe Set-up Operator				C							
Inspector, General							C		C		
Buffing-Machine Operator			C								
Pantograph-Machine Set-up Operator						C	C				
Drill-Press Operator						C					
Lathe Operator, Production	S					S					

C = Competitive Employment; S = Sheltered Employment

Other jobs in this division:

- Salvage Engineer
- Experimental Mechanic
- Machinist, Automotive
- Tool-and-Die Maker
- Gear Inspector
- Grinder Operator, Tool
- Milling-Machine Operator, Production
- Threading-Machine Operator
- Screwmaker, Automatic

Opening jobs in this division:

Entry to these jobs is usually gained through apprenticeship programs or on-the-job training. Workers who are unable to undergo such training or to manipulate objects would be excluded from these jobs. Those with mobility handicaps may be aided by providing mobility devices or by redesigning the work place. Public attitudes may interfere with obtaining a job or may contribute to false expectations of worker performance.

61

METAL WORKING
OCCUPATIONS,
N.E.C.

This division includes occupations, not elsewhere classified, concerned with shaping and conditioning metal by rolling, forging, extruding, drawing out, punching, shearing, blanking, and press working. (DOT, 4th Edition, p. 513)

Jobs held by handicapped workers:

D.O.T. JOB TITLE	MENTALLY RETARDED— Trainable	MENTALLY RETARDED— Severe & Profound	EMOTIONALLY DISTURBED	MULTIPLY HANDICAPPED	EPILEPSY	CEREBRAL PALSY	PARAPLEGIC	QUADRIPLEGIC	OTHER ORTHOPEDIC	SEVERE HEALTH	SEVERE NEUROLOGICAL
Machine Operator I									C		
Bending-Machine Operator I										C	
Machine Operator II	C										
Machine Helper			C,S	C			S				

C = Competitive Employment; S = Sheltered Workshop

Other jobs in this division:

- Blacksmith Helper
- Hydraulic Operator
- Spike-Machine Operator
- Coiler Operator
- Draw-Bench Operator
- Ironworker-Machine Operator
- Brake Operator
- Forming-Roll Operator I
- Embossing-Machine Operator

Opening jobs in this division:

Entry to these jobs, as with metal working occupations in division 60, is usually gained by apprenticeship programs or on-the-job training. Handicapped workers who are unable to undergo such training or to manipulate objects would be excluded from these jobs. Those with mobility handicaps may be aided by mobility devices or by redesigning the work place, although some work places would require such extensive redesign as to make this option impractical. Public attitudes may interfere with obtaining a job or may contribute to false expectations of worker performance.

<table>
<tr><td rowspan="2" style="width:30%">62/63

MECHANICS AND
MACHINERY
REPAIRERS</td><td>This division includes occupations concerned with installing, inspecting, testing, repairing, rebuilding, and maintaining in efficient operating condition all types of engines and a wide variety of mechanical equipment designed for general or specific application in domestic, commercial, industrial, and agricultural activities. Occupations in this division typically require knowledge of the structural and functional characteristics of specific machines or types of machines, and include such tasks as locating and drilling holes, alining structural and moving parts, and occasionally operating machine tools to remove excess metal from semifinished or repaired parts. Occupations concerned with assembling new or rebuilt heavy machines, such as turbines and presses in the machine shop or erection shop, involving close tolerance machining and hand finishing of castings and other machine parts are included in Division 60. Occupations concerned with machine setup and adjustment only are included in groups covering operation of the same machines. (DOT, 4th Edition, p. 536)</td></tr>
</table>

Jobs held by handicapped workers:

D.O.T. JOB TITLE	MENTALLY RETARDED— Trainable	MENTALLY RETARDED— Severe & Profound	EMOTIONALLY DISTURBED	MULTIPLY HANDICAPPED	EPILEPSY	CEREBRAL PALSY	PARAPLEGIC	QUADRIPLEGIC	OTHER ORTHOPEDIC	SEVERE HEALTH	SEVERE NEUROLOGICAL
Engine Repairer, Service	C		C	C	C		C				
Automobile-Mechanic Helper			C								
Used Car Renovator	C					C					
Repairer, Pump							C				
Repairer II							C				
Refrigeration-Mechanic Helper				C							

C = Competitive Employment

Other jobs in this division:

- Automobile Tester
- Air-Conditioning Mechanic
- Braker Repairer
- Motorcycle Repairer
- Maintenance Mechanic Helper
- Valve Repairer
- Assembly Technician
- Parts Salvager
- Coin-Machine-Service Repairer

Opening jobs in this division:

This occupational division consists of jobs that involve a variety of skills. Entry into these jobs is usually through apprenticeships which provide 2 to 6 years of on-the-job training and trade instruction. Opportunities for opening jobs to handicapped workers include adapting the work place, redesigning jobs to suit the capabilities of handicapped workers, and utilizing special tools, mobility aids, and communication devices. Negative public attitudes may be overcome by involving business, labor, and industry in training and placement. Once handicapped workers prove their productivity, attitude barriers should fall. Special needs programs in vocational training schools will become more and more useful.

This division includes occupations concerned with reproducing data or designs by mechanical transfer of ink or dye to the surface of materials with the aid of type, plates, rolls, and the like. Includes the preparation of type and plate for machines and mechanical bookbinding. (DOT, 4th Edition, p. 566)

Jobs held by handicapped workers:

D.O.T. JOB TITLE	MENTALLY RETARDED— Trainable	MENTALLY RETARDED— Severe & Profound	EMOTIONALLY DISTURBED	MULTIPLY HANDICAPPED	EPILEPSY	CEREBRAL PALSY	PARAPLEGIC	QUADRIPLEGIC	OTHER ORTHOPEDIC	SEVERE HEALTH	SEVERE NEUROLOGICAL
Collator	S	C,S	C,S	S							
Offset Press Operator I							C				
Silk-Screen Printer, Machine						S					
Bindery Worker	C										
Offset-Press Operator II			C				C				
Printer		S		C							

C = Competitive Employment; S = Sheltered Workshop

Other jobs in this division:

- Typesetting-Machine Tender
- Engraving-Press Operator
- Printer, Plastic
- Press Helper
- Cloth Printer
- Wallpaper Printer
- Plate Finisher
- Embosser
- Sign Writer, Machine
- Sample-Book Maker

Opening jobs in this division:

Persons who have had some experience working with machines in a school or work environment are frequently preferred for these jobs. Mainstream vocational education, apprenticeship programs, and on-the-job training are common methods by which workers attain competence. Physical and mobility requirements will vary greatly depending upon the machine to be operated and the nature of the controls. Controls may be modified for the individual handicapped worker. Communication barriers may not be a serious obstacle once skill is obtained. Special training prior to on-the-job training may be advisable to ensure the handicapped worker's confidence and to increase his or her experience.

This division includes occupations concerned with shaping wooden parts or products by removing excess material from stock or objects, primarily by such means as cutting, boring, abrading, milling, and planing. Includes laying out, job setting, repairing, fitting, and assembling. Includes machining cork and corncob pipes. (DOT, 4th Edition, p. 578)

Jobs held by handicapped workers:

D.O.T. JOB TITLE	MENTALLY RETARDED— Trainable	MENTALLY RETARDED— Severe & Profound	EMOTIONALLY DISTURBED	MULTIPLY HANDICAPPED	EPILEPSY	CEREBRAL PALSY	PARAPLEGIC	QUADRIPLEGIC	OTHER ORTHOPEDIC	SEVERE HEALTH	SEVERE NEUROLOGICAL
Cabinetmaker			C	C							

C = Competitive Employment

Other jobs in this division:

- Patternmaker, Wood   • Hat-Block Maker   • Molding Sander   • Wood-Carving-Machine Operator
- Framer   • Head Sawyer   • Sawmill Worker   • Buzzsaw-Operator Helper   • Barrel Assembler
- Lumber Straightener

Opening jobs in this division:

Entry to these jobs is usually gained through apprenticeship programs or on-the-job training. Lifting and other physical requirements vary, and many jobs are beyond the capabilities of those with severe orthopedic handicaps. Communication disorders should be manageable in most cases using one or more of the strategies discussed in this book.

69

MACHINE TRADES
OCCUPATIONS,
N.E.C.

This division includes occupations, not elsewhere classified, concerned with feeding, tending, operating, controlling, and setting up machines to work various materials and products. (DOT, 4th Edition, p. 623)

Jobs held by handicapped workers:

D.O.T. JOB TITLE	MENTALLY RETARDED—Trainable	MENTALLY RETARDED—Severe & Profound	EMOTIONALLY DISTURBED	MULTIPLY HANDICAPPED	EPILEPSY	CEREBRAL PALSY	PARAPLEGIC	QUADRIPLEGIC	OTHER ORTHOPEDIC	SEVERE HEALTH	SEVERE NEUROLOGICAL
Assembly-Press Operator	S										
Electric-Sealing-Machine Operator			C								
Kick-Press Operator	C			S							
Stapler, Machine	C	S									
Eyelet-Machine Operator		S	C	S			S				
Oiler	C										

C = Competitive Employment; S = Sheltered Workshop

Other jobs in this division:

- Machine Setter
- Hide Splitter
- Bias-Machine Operator
- Bowling-Ball Finisher
- Laminator I (leather prod.)
- Tube Splicer (rubber tire & tube)
- Abestos-Wire Finisher
- Insulating-Machine Operator
- Light-Bulb Assembler

Opening jobs in this division:

Persons who have had some experience working with machines in a school or work environment are frequently preferred for these jobs. On-the-job training is the most common method by which workers attain competence. Physical and mobility requirements for these jobs will vary greatly depending upon the machine to be operated and the nature of the controls. Intellectual demands vary greatly as a function of the degree of supervisory responsibility and type of machine operated. Controls may be modified for the benefit of the individual handicapped worker. Communication barriers may not be a serious obstacle once skill is obtained. Special training prior to on-the-job training may be advisable to ensure the handicapped worker's confidence and to increase his or her experience.

This division includes occupations, not elsewhere classified, concerned with fabricating, assembling, and repairing or reconditioning products primarily made of metal, but may include parts of plastic or other materials. Also includes products usually made of metal, such as certain tools, but sometimes made of a substitute metallic-type material, the fabrication of which involves use of tooling and techniques similar to metalworking. (DOT, 4th Edition, p. 651)

Jobs held by handicapped workers:

D.O.T. JOB TITLE	MENTALLY RETARDED—Trainable	MENTALLY RETARDED—Severe & Profound	EMOTIONALLY DISTURBED	MULTIPLY HANDICAPPED	EPILEPSY	CEREBRAL PALSY	PARAPLEGIC	QUADRIPLEGIC	OTHER ORTHOPEDIC	SEVERE HEALTH	SEVERE NEUROLOGICAL
Locksmith										C	
Lapper, Hand Tool									C		
Laborer, Grinding and Polishing										C	
Assembler, Production				C,S							
Assembler			C	C						C	

C = Competitive Employment; S = Sheltered Workshop

Other jobs in this division:

- Jeweler
- Silversmith
- Goldbeater
- Ring Maker
- Mesh Cutter
- Etcher
- Buffer I
- Metal Finisher
- Fabric Stretcher
- Gold Reclaimer
- Cleaner and Polisher

Opening jobs in this division:

All of the jobs in this division are done at tables and benches, so routine accessibility modifications should make the work place accessible to the orthopedically handicapped. Some require considerable judgment or the ability to understand technical instructions, while others do not. Precision requirements vary substantially. Those with severe upper limb involvement may be excluded from some jobs but could perform others with assistive devices. Intellectual demands also vary greatly. Retarded workers may be able to do some of these jobs if powerful training techniques are employed and some job redesign is undertaken. Generally, speech and hearing deficits should present few problems once proficiency is gained in the job skills.

FABRICATION
AND REPAIR OF
SCIENTIFIC, MEDICAL,
PHOTOGRAPHIC,
OPTICAL, HOROLOGICAL,
AND RELATED PRODUCTS

This division includes occupations concerned with assembling, fabricating, and repairing scientific, engineering, and medical equipment, photographic and optical goods, clocks, and watches, and related products including fabrication of precision optical and ophthalmic lenses, using specialized handtools and bench-type machines. (DOT, 4th Edition, p. 668)

Jobs held by handicapped workers:

D.O.T. JOB TITLE	MENTALLY RETARDED— Trainable	MENTALLY RETARDED— Severe & Profound	EMOTIONALLY DISTURBED	MULTIPLY HANDICAPPED	EPILEPSY	CEREBRAL PALSY	PARAPLEGIC	QUADRIPLEGIC	OTHER ORTHOPEDIC	SEVERE HEALTH	SEVERE NEUROLOGICAL
Watch Repairer										C	
Dental-Laboratory-Technician Apprentice									C		
Dental Technician, Crown and Bridge			C				C			C	
Optician Apprentice									C		
Lens Polisher, Hand			C		C						
Assembler, Gold Fram									C		
Contact-Lens-Curve Grinder					C						
Bellows Assembler				C,S							

C = Competitive Employment; S = Sheltered Workshop

Other jobs in this division:

- Instrument Repairer
- Gas-Meter Mechanic
- Parking-Meter Servicer
- Orthodonic Technician
- Watch Assembler
- Jewel-Inserter
- Eyeglass-Lens Cutter
- Lens Examiner
- Hearing-Aid Repairer

Opening jobs in this division:

Most of the jobs in this division do not require heavy lifting, and most can be performed without moving from work station to work station or crawling under equipment. Therefore, accessibility modifications to allow the orthopedically impaired worker to reach the work place should make these jobs possible for many. Precise manipulation of small, delicate objects is required on many of these jobs. People with poor upper limb coordination are, therefore, excluded from many jobs, although assistive devices may be useful in certain cases and the possibility may be worth exploring. Intellectual demands are fairly high in most jobs as the worker often has to follow engineering diagrams or other technical instructions. Speech and hearing deficits should generally present only minor barriers once proficiency is achieved.

This division includes occupations concerned with assembling, fabricating, or repairing equipment, components, and parts for equipment to transmit, control, or convert electrical power; signaling and detection equipment; and home radios, television sets, and phonographs. (DOT, 4th Edition, p. 691)

Jobs held by handicapped workers:

D.O.T. JOB TITLE	MENTALLY RETARDED—Trainable	MENTALLY RETARDED—Severe & Profound	EMOTIONALLY DISTURBED	MULTIPLY HANDICAPPED	EPILEPSY	CEREBRAL PALSY	PARAPLEGIC	QUADRIPLEGIC	OTHER ORTHOPEDIC	SEVERE HEALTH	SEVERE NEUROLOGICAL
Television-and-Radio Repairer			C	C	C	C	C				
Electrical-Appliance Repairer			C								
Electronics Assembler			S					C	C	C	C
Appliance Repairer			C	C							
Assembler, Electrical AccessoriesI			C								

C = Competitive Employment; S = Sheltered Workshop

Other jobs in this division:

- Electric-Motor Repairer
- Electronic Tester
- Plug Wirer
- Battery Repairer
- Dry-Cell Tester
- Battery-Parts Assembler
- Cable Maker
- Audio-Video Repairer
- Street-Light-Repairer Helper

Opening jobs in this division:

A large number of jobs in this division are already available to severely handicapped workers with a variety of handicapping conditions. Severe orthopedic handicaps, which limit the manipulation of objects and tools, may prohibit work in some of these jobs, particularly those in which heavy electrical equipment is involved or in which equipment must be repaired or installed in locations that are hard to reach. Communication handicaps are probably not critical, providing they can be circumvented by sign language and communication devices.

73

FABRICATION AND
REPAIR OF PRODUCTS
MADE FROM ASSORTED
MATERIALS

This division includes occupations concerned with shaping, fitting, trimming, assembling, joining, finishing, and repairing products made from combinations of such materials as metal, wood, plastics, rubber, fabric, and paper. (DOT, 4th Edition, p. 709)

Jobs held by handicapped workers:

D.O.T. JOB TITLE	MENTALLY RETARDED— Trainable	MENTALLY RETARDED— Severe & Profound	EMOTIONALLY DISTURBED	MULTIPLY HANDICAPPED	EPILEPSY	CEREBRAL PALSY	PARAPLEGIC	QUADRIPLEGIC	OTHER ORTHOPEDIC	SEVERE HEALTH	SEVERE NEUROLOGICAL
Inspector, Bullet Slugs									C		
Wig Maker					C						
Racket Stringer	C	S									
Broommaker				S	S						
Sander-and-Buffer	C		C								
Wire Cutter	C,S										
Linker (jewelry)				C							
Stone Setter							C,S				
Assembler (ammunitions)							C				
Assembler, Small Products	C						C				

C = Competitive Employment; S = Sheltered Workshop

Other jobs in this division:

- Accordion Maker
- Piano Technician
- Violin Maker, Hand
- Tuner, Percussion
- Musical-String Maker
- Toy Assembler
- Golf-Club Repairer
- Sports-Equipment Repairer
- Bead Stringer
- Stone Setter (jewelry)

Opening jobs in this division:

This division comprises a wide variety of largely benchwork occupations. A great many of these jobs can be performed by the orthopedically impaired once architectural barriers have been removed. In addition, work station modification and assistive devices may be required. Intellectual demands vary greatly, and a few jobs may be within the reach of the retarded with job redesign and specialized training programs.

This division includes occupations concerned with fabricating and repairing complete wooden articles, or subassemblies of wooden structures, involving the use of woodworking handtools and power tools. (DOT, 4th Edition, p. 749)

Jobs held by handicapped workers:

D.O.T. JOB TITLE	MENTALLY RETARDED— Trainable	MENTALLY RETARDED— Severe & Profound	EMOTIONALLY DISTURBED	MULTIPLY HANDICAPPED	EPILEPSY	CEREBRAL PALSY	PARAPLEGIC	QUADRIPLEGIC	OTHER ORTHOPEDIC	SEVERE HEALTH	SEVERE NEUROLOGICAL
Furniture Finisher	C			C			S				
Sander, Machine	C,S										
Caner I				S							
Woodworking-Shop Hand	C	S									

C = Competitive Employment; S = Sheltered Workshop

Other jobs in this division:

- Carver, Hand
- Smoking-Pipe Maker
- Glued Wood Tester
- Door Assembler
- Cabinet Assembler
- Wicker Worker
- Weaver (basketry)
- Frame Trimmer
- Veneer Matcher

Opening jobs in this division:

This division includes benchwork occupations that offer many opportunities for the orthopedically handicapped once accessibility modifications are made. Work place redesign and various aids and devices may increase the range of possible jobs for those with upper limb involvement. Some of these jobs can be done by the mentally retarded, but carefully structured training programs may be required to help them gain the requisite skills.

<table>
<tr><td>77</td></tr>
<tr><td>FABRICATION AND
REPAIR OF SAND,
STONE, CLAY, AND
GLASS PRODUCTS</td></tr>
</table>

This division includes occupations concerned with handcraft and related activities involving specialized handtools and power tools used in grading, cutting, and polishing precious or semiprecious stones, including natural or synthetic gems, jewel bearings, and diamond wiredrawing dies; cutting and polishing ornamental and structural stone; forming, decorating, and finishing porcelain, pottery, tiles, and other ceramic products; molding, shaping, and decorating artistic and laboratory glassware, pressed lenses, and other handmade glass products; and producing commercial or industrial abrasives. (DOT, 4th Edition, p. 759)

Jobs held by handicapped workers:

D.O.T. JOB TITLE	MENTALLY RETARDED— Trainable	MENTALLY RETARDED— Severe & Profound	EMOTIONALLY DISTURBED	MULTIPLY HANDICAPPED	EPILEPSY	CEREBRAL PALSY	PARAPLEGIC	QUADRIPLEGIC	OTHER ORTHOPEDIC	SEVERE HEALTH	SEVERE NEUROLOGICAL
Grinding Wheel Inspector								C			
Dipper	C										

C = Competitive Employment

Other jobs in this division:

- Diamond Expert
- Gem Cutter
- Phonograph-Needle-Tip Maker
- Stone Carver
- Beveler
- Glass Blower
- Plaster-Die Maker
- Glass Decorator
- Glass Cutter
- Concrete Sculptor

Opening jobs in this division:

This division includes benchwork occupations that are accessible to many physically handicapped once appropriate modifications are made and aids provided. Also, some of the jobs are within reach of the retarded, given sufficient training and, in some cases, job redesign.

78

FABRICATION AND REPAIR OF TEXTILE, LEATHER AND RELATED PRODUCTS

This division includes occupations concerned with laying out, marking, and cutting materials; hand-sewing of machine-sewing parts of mass-produced products, such as drapes, slip covers, sheets, pillowcases, and ready-to-wear apparel; fitting and stitching made-to-measure garments and accessories; hand knitting complete garments, garment parts, or accessories; hand weaving and embroidering to embellish or repair garments and accessories; fabricating footwear, except molded rubber and plastics; and other activities concerned with fabricating or repairing garments, canvas goods, house furnishings, and related products. (DOT, 4th Edition, p. 771)

Jobs held by handicapped workers:

D.O.T. JOB TITLE	MENTALLY RETARDED—Trainable	MENTALLY RETARDED—Severe & Profound	EMOTIONALLY DISTURBED	MULTIPLY HANDICAPPED	EPILEPSY	CEREBRAL PALSY	PARAPLEGIC	QUADRIPLEGIC	OTHER ORTHOPEDIC	SEVERE HEALTH	SEVERE NEUROLOGICAL
Furniture Upholsterer				C		C					
Shop Tailor				C							
Upholstery Sewer	C,S	S	C,S	S			C,S				
Upholstery Repairer										C	
Leather Worker				C							
Stapler, Hand		S								C	
Clipper		S									
Automobile Upholsterer			C				C				

C = Competitive Employment; S = Sheltered Workshop

Other jobs in this division:

- Box-Spring Maker
- Cushion Maker I
- Mattress Finisher
- Rug Clipper
- Cutter Helper
- Fabric Worker
- Hat Maker
- Dressmaker
- Hemmer, Blindstitch
- Mender

Opening jobs in this division:

Comments that apply to other benchwork occupations (divisions 73, 76, and 77) also apply to jobs in this division.

79

BENCH WORK
OCCUPATIONS, N.E.C.

This division includes bench work occupations, not elsewhere classified. (DOT, 4th Edition, p. 801)

Jobs held by handicapped workers:

D.O.T. JOB TITLE	MENTALLY RETARDED— Trainable	MENTALLY RETARDED— Severe & Profound	EMOTIONALLY DISTURBED	MULTIPLY HANDICAPPED	EPILEPSY	CEREBRAL PALSY	PARAPLEGIC	QUADRIPLEGIC	OTHER ORTHOPEDIC	SEVERE HEALTH	SEVERE NEUROLOGICAL
Gluer			C								

C = Competitive Employment

Other jobs in this division:

- Tobacco Blender
- Cigar Maker
- Candy Cutter, Hand
- Box Maker, Paperboard
- Paper-Novelty Maker
- Punchboard Assembler I
- Coverer, Looseleaf Binder

Opening jobs in this division:

See divisions 73, 76, 77, and 78 for remarks that apply here as well.

80
METAL FABRICATING, N.E.C.

This division includes occupations concerned with fabricating, erecting, and repairing building frames and ornamental metalwork, bridges, trestles, marine craft and structures, boilers, storage tanks, drilling rigs, towers, and other structures generally assembled from heavy structural plates, beams, and castings; fitting and assembling vehicle bodies, ariframes, prefabricated door casings and window frames, air ducts, and other structural units assembled from stock or preformed sheet metal and structural shapes; and assembling or repairing boats, automobile bodies, and other structural units partially or entirely constructed of rigid plastics or fiberglass. (DOT, 4th Edition, p. 805)

Jobs held by handicapped workers:

D.O.T. JOB TITLE	MENTALLY RETARDED— Trainable	MENTALLY RETARDED— Severe & Profound	EMOTIONALLY DISTURBED	MULTIPLY HANDICAPPED	EPILEPSY	CEREBRAL PALSY	PARAPLEGIC	QUADRIPLEGIC	OTHER ORTHOPEDIC	SEVERE HEALTH	SEVERE NEUROLOGICAL
Fitter (machine shop)									C		
Layout Worker II			C								
Repairer, General				C							

C = Competitive Employment

Other jobs in this division:

- Riveter
- Assembler, Mining Machinery
- Sheet-Metal Worker
- Boilermaker
- Rigger, Apprentice
- Utility Worker, Line Assembly
- Shipfitter
- Assembler, Automobile
- Lay-Out Worker I

Opening jobs in this division:

Most jobs in this division require heavy physical activity, and severely orthopedically handicapped people will not be able to do them. Speech and hearing deficiencies should prove manageable on most jobs once basic communication techniques are taught to supervisors and co-workers.

<table>
<tr><td rowspan="2" colspan="4">81</td></tr>
</table>

81

WELDERS, CUTTERS,
AND RELATED
OCCUPATIONS

This division includes occupations primarily concerned with joining, surfacing, or otherwise fabricating or repairing structures or parts of metal or other weldable material, such as plastic or glass, applying the following welding or cutting processes: arc; gas; resistance; solid state (friction, ultrasonic, cold, explosion, diffusion); and other processes, such as electroslag, electron beam, induction, thermit, and laser beam. Welders in this division are distinguished from workers using welding equipment in other divisions by their knowledge of and experience in welding technology and in being primarily concerned with the equipment and technology of welding. Workers classified in other divisions may use welding equipment, but their knowledge and experience are primarily in assembly or repair techniques. For example, welders who work on storage batteries can be found in Division 72. (DOT, 4th Edition, p. 824)

Jobs held by handicapped workers:

D.O.T. JOB TITLE	MENTALLY RETARDED— Trainable	MENTALLY RETARDED— Severe & Profound	EMOTIONALLY DISTURBED	MULTIPLY HANDICAPPED	EPILEPSY	CEREBRAL PALSY	PARAPLEGIC	QUADRIPLEGIC	OTHER ORTHOPEDIC	SEVERE HEALTH	SEVERE NEUROLOGICAL
Welder, Arc			C	C							
Welder Helper	C										

C = Competitive Employment

Other jobs in this division:

- Blazer, Furnace
- Laser-Beam-Machine Operator
- Thermal Cutter, Hand
- Lead Burner
- Machine Helper
- Machine Feeder

Opening jobs in this division:

The heavy physical demands of these jobs constitute a substantial barrier to most people with severe orthopedic impairments. Some of these may be overcome using work station redesign or special aids and devices, but most will probably prove insurmountable. Hearing and speech impairments should be manageable on many jobs once the requisite job skills are acquired.

ELECTRICAL
ASSEMBLING,
INSTALLING,
AND REPAIRING
OCCUPATIONS

This division includes occupations concerned with assembling, installing, erecting, and repairing electrical equipment and related structures designed for electric power generation, transmission, and distribution; communication, signaling, and object detection; process control, fire control, and data processing; transportation and materials-handling; heating, air conditioning, refrigeration, and illumination; and other industrial, commercial, and domestic electrical applications. (DOT, 4th Edition, p. 830)

Jobs held by handicapped workers:

D.O.T. JOB TITLE	MENTALLY RETARDED— Trainable	MENTALLY RETARDED— Severe & Profound	EMOTIONALLY DISTURBED	MULTIPLY HANDICAPPED	EPILEPSY	CEREBRAL PALSY	PARAPLEGIC	QUADRIPLEGIC	OTHER ORTHOPEDIC	SEVERE HEALTH	SEVERE NEUROLOGICAL
Electrician			C								
Laboratory Helper			C								

C = Competitive Employment

Other jobs in this division:

● Relay Technician   ● Television-Cable Installer   ● Line Repairer   ● Utilities Service Investigator
● Voltage Tester   ● Transmission Tester   ● Television Installer   ● Neon-Sign Servicer   ● Cable Splicer

Opening jobs in this division:

Most of these jobs make heavy physical demands that would be too difficult for severely orthopedically people to meet, even with assistive devices. Many communications handicaps can be overcome with various aids or with basic communications training for co-workers.

PAINTING,
PLASTERING,
WATERPROOFING,
CEMENTING, AND
RELATED OCCUPATIONS

This division includes occupations concerned with preparing surfaces to be covered; mixing coating ingredients; erecting scaffolding; and applying protective or decorative materials, such as cement, concrete, lacquer, paint, plaster, and wallpaper, to structural surfaces by spraying, brushing, troweling or hand-pressing. (DOT, 4th Edition, p. 846)

Jobs held by handicapped workers:

D.O.T. JOB TITLE	MENTALLY RETARDED— Trainable	MENTALLY RETARDED— Severe & Profound	EMOTIONALLY DISTURBED	MULTIPLY HANDICAPPED	EPILEPSY	CEREBRAL PALSY	PARAPLEGIC	QUADRIPLEGIC	OTHER ORTHOPEDIC	SEVERE HEALTH	SEVERE NEUROLOGICAL
Painter Apprentice, Automotive							C				

C = Competitive Employment

Other jobs in this division:

- Glass Tinter
- Paperhanger
- Plasterer
- Dry-Wall Applicator
- Stucco Mason
- Cement Mason

Opening jobs in this division:

Intensive on-the-job training in techniques and methods is the best way to become qualified in this field. Apprenticeship programs and work experience in jobs of lesser complexity are also helpful. Mobility handicaps are serious barriers, although dispatcher and some other supervisory jobs are possibilities. Communication handicaps may be aided by appropriate devices.

86

CONSTRUCTION
OCCUPATIONS,
N.E.C.

This division includes craft and noncraft occupations, not elsewhere classified, concerned with building and repairing structures. (DOT, 4th Edition, p. 854)

Jobs held by handicapped workers:

D.O.T. JOB TITLE	MENTALLY RETARDED—Trainable	MENTALLY RETARDED—Severe & Profound	EMOTIONALLY DISTURBED	MULTIPLY HANDICAPPED	EPILEPSY	CEREBRAL PALSY	PARAPLEGIC	QUADRIPLEGIC	OTHER ORTHOPEDIC	SEVERE HEALTH	SEVERE NEUROLOGICAL
Carpet Layer										C	
Carpenter			C								
Bricklayer			C								
Carpenter, Rough			C	C							
Construction Worker I			C								
Painter Helper		S		C							
Carpenter Helper, Maintenance	C			C							
Laborer, Carpentry	C,S		C						C		
Bricklayer Helper				C							
Stonemason Helper				C							

C = Competitive Employment; S = Sheltered Workshop

Other jobs in this division:

- Acoustical Carpenter
- Boatbuilder, Wood
- Marble Setter
- Tile Setter
- Pipe Fitter
- Coppersmith
- Plumber
- Floor-Layer
- Glass Installer
- Sign Erector

Opening jobs in this division:

Major barriers and the strategies for overcoming them are much the same as in division 82.

89
STRUCTURAL WORK OCCUPATIONS, N.E.C.

This division includes occupations, not elsewhere classified, concerned with structural work. (DOT, 4th Edition, p. 872)

Jobs held by handicapped workers:

D.O.T. JOB TITLE	MENTALLY RETARDED—Trainable	MENTALLY RETARDED—Severe & Profound	EMOTIONALLY DISTURBED	MULTIPLY HANDICAPPED	EPILEPSY	CEREBRAL PALSY	PARAPLEGIC	QUADRIPLEGIC	OTHER ORTHOPEDIC	SEVERE HEALTH	SEVERE NEUROLOGICAL
Maintenance Repairer, Building			C							C	C

C = Competitive Employment

Other jobs in this division:

- Pipe Cleaner
- Dock Hand
- Swimming-Pool Servicer
- Chimney Sweep
- Furnace Cleaner
- Tank Cleaner
- Pipeliner
- Window Repairer
- Decorator, Street and Building

Opening jobs in this division:

Major barriers and the strategies for overcoming them are much the same as in division 82.

This division includes occupations concerned with transporting cargo over highways, city streets, or within compounds of industrial, construction, or mining areas, by driving vehicles powered by gasoline, diesel, propane, or related fuels, or electricity. (DOT, 4th Edition, p. 877)

Jobs held by handicapped workers:

D.O.T. JOB TITLE	MENTALLY RETARDED— Trainable	MENTALLY RETARDED— Severe & Profound	EMOTIONALLY DISTURBED	MULTIPLY HANDICAPPED	EPILEPSY	CEREBRAL PALSY	PARAPLEGIC	QUADRIPLEGIC	OTHER ORTHOPEDIC	SEVERE HEALTH	SEVERE NEUROLOGICAL
Truck Driver, Light			C							C	
Garbage Collector	C										

C = Competitive Employment

Other jobs in this division:

- Dump-Truck Driver
- Milk Driver
- Van Driver
- Food-Service Driver

Opening jobs in this division:

Applicants for jobs in this division must be able to handle light to very heavy loads. Many nonhandicapped people can qualify for these jobs, so personal traits such as reliability, honesty, and industry will be important considerations. Workers with orthopedic handicaps will not be able to handle many of these jobs. Communication handicaps need not be serious barriers if appropiate strategies are used to manage them. Attitudinal problems, if any, should decline as a handicapped worker demonstrates competence.

91

TRANSPORTATION OCCUPATIONS, N.E.C.

This division includes occupations, not elsewhere classified, concerned with moving people or materials by means of automotive and railway vehicles, aircraft, freshwater or seagoing vessels, pipes, and pumps. Includes loading bulk materials into conveyances; directing course of carrier; routing materials; minor repair and maintenance of carriers; and related activities. (DOT, 4th Edition, p. 879)

Jobs held by handicapped workers:

D.O.T. JOB TITLE	MENTALLY RETARDED—Trainable	MENTALLY RETARDED—Severe & Profound	EMOTIONALLY DISTURBED	MULTIPLY HANDICAPPED	EPILEPSY	CEREBRAL PALSY	PARAPLEGIC	QUADRIPLEGIC	OTHER ORTHOPEDIC	SEVERE HEALTH	SEVERE NEUROLOGICAL
Automobile-Service-Station Attendant	C			C							
Chauffeur									C	C	
Parking Lot Attendant	C,S					C		C		C	
Cleaner II (unspecified)		C	C								
Loader I (truck)	C										
Loader Helper	C										
Car Cleaner	C										

C = Competitive Employment; S = Sheltered Workshop

Other jobs in this division:

- Conductor, Yard
- Locomotive Engineer
- Baggage Handler
- Track Oiler
- Ferryboat Operator
- Deckhand
- Airport Attendant
- Bus Driver
- Gas-and-Oil Servicer
- Steam Cleaner

Opening jobs in this division:

Jobs in this division make a wide variety of demands, and any of the strategies for overcoming barriers may prove necessary.

92

PACKAGING AND
MATERIALS HANDLING
OCCUPATIONS

This division includes occupations concerned with preparing and arranging materials and products in bulk and nonbulk forms for distribution or storage; moving and loading or unloading equipment, materials, and products; operating or tending filling, packing, and wrapping machines or conveyors; driving forklifts, lumber carriers, and related material-handling machinery and equipment; and using scoops, handtrucks, and wheelbarrows to load and move materials. (DOT, 4th Edition, p. 891)

Jobs held by handicapped workers:

D.O.T. JOB TITLE	MENTALLY RETARDED—Trainable	MENTALLY RETARDED—Severe & Profound	EMOTIONALLY DISTURBED	MULTIPLY HANDICAPPED	EPILEPSY	CEREBRAL PALSY	PARAPLEGIC	QUADRIPLEGIC	OTHER ORTHOPEDIC	SEVERE HEALTH	SEVERE NEUROLOGICAL
Packager, Machine						C			C		
Baling-Machine Tender	S										
Bagger	C										
Marker II	C	S		S						S	
Packager, Hand	C,S	C,S	C,S	C,S	C	C	C				
Paper Inserter	C			S							
Stenciler	S										
Laborer, Stores	C				C	C			C		
Laborer, Salvage	C										

C = Competitive Employment; S = Sheltered Workshop

Other jobs in this division:

- Cotton Baler
- Carter
- Label Coder
- Cigarette-Package Examiner
- Can Inspector
- Sample Worker
- Cement Loader
- Conveyor Operator
- Timber Packer

Opening jobs in this division:

Physical handicaps are the most serious barrier in this division. Practically all jobs require upper limb strength and dexterity, and bulk packaging and shipping usually require the worker to be ambulatory. Work station redesign and special aids may help to open nonbulk packaging and shipping jobs to those with upper limb involvement. In most jobs, communication handicaps can be managed using one or more of the strategies discussed in this book. Many jobs are already held by the retarded, and powerful training procedures coupled with job redesign could open more.

This division includes occupations concerned with generation, transmission, and distribution of electricity; generation and distribution of steam for heat and power, including marine propulsion; generation of utility gas, and storage and distribution of natural and manufactured gas for power, illumination, or heating purposes; filtration, purification, and distribution of water for domestic, commercial, or industrial consumption; and collection, treatment, and disposal of sewage and refuse. (DOT, 4th Edition, p. 919)

Jobs held by handicapped workers:

D.O.T. JOB TITLE	MENTALLY RETARDED— Trainable	MENTALLY RETARDED— Severe & Profound	EMOTIONALLY DISTURBED	MULTIPLY HANDICAPPED	EPILEPSY	CEREBRAL PALSY	PARAPLEGIC	QUADRIPLEGIC	OTHER ORTHOPEDIC	SEVERE HEALTH	SEVERE NEUROLOGICAL
Dispatcher, Service							C				
Stationary Engineer			C								

C = Competitive Employment

Other jobs in this division:

- Refrigerating Engineer
- Switchboard Operator
- Power Operator
- Waste-Treatment Operator
- Snow Shoveler
- Electric Powerline Examiner
- Service Representative
- Facility Examiner

Opening jobs in this division:

Many of these jobs require heavy physical labor or working in environments difficult for those with severe orthopedic impairments to negotiate. The significance of communications varies widely, but strategies discussed under communications barriers are frequently required. Many jobs involve significant danger, and careful training and supervision should be provided if the retarded are to be employed. Also, many jobs require an intellectual sophistication beyond the ability of retarded workers.

97

GRAPHIC ART WORK

This division includes occupations concerned with handsetting text or display type; making and mounting plates of line or continuous tone illustrations; assembling hand- or machine-set type, plates, and spacing material to make up pages and forms; reproducing type, illustrations, pages, and forms by photoengraving, lighographic process, electrotyping, or sterotyping to make plates for printing presses; copying lettering, lines, or designs, and retouching artwork; etching or engraving printing rollers; developing and printing film and prints; bookbinding; and related graphic arts activities. Occupations concerned with cold type typesetting and word processing are found in Division 20. (DOT, 4th Edition, p. 931)

Jobs held by handicapped workers:

D.O.T. JOB TITLE	MENTALLY RETARDED—Trainable	MENTALLY RETARDED—Severe & Profound	EMOTIONALLY DISTURBED	MULTIPLY HANDICAPPED	EPILEPSY	CEREBRAL PALSY	PARAPLEGIC	QUADRIPLEGIC	OTHER ORTHOPEDIC	SEVERE HEALTH	SEVERE NEUROLOGICAL
Letterer				C							
Reproduction Technician				C						C	
Photo Checker and Assembler				C						C	
Engraver I				C							
Blueprinting-Machine Operator						C					
Pantographer								C			
Screen Printer		S	S	S			S	S			
Photographic Finisher I									C		
Print-Shop Helper	C										
X-Ray-Developing-Machine Operator				C							

C = Competitive Employment; S = Sheltered Workshop

Other jobs in this division:

- Etcher, Hand
- Photoengraver
- Sketch Maker
- Job Printer
- Proofsheet Corrector
- Microfiche Duplicator
- Projection Printer
- Film Laboratory Technician

Opening jobs in this division:

A large number of these jobs are already available for the severely handicapped, both in competitive employment and in sheltered workshops that have been specially designed for them. Severe orthopedic handicaps, which limit the manipulation of objects and tools, may make some of these jobs beyond their ability. Communication handicaps are probably not critical, providing they can be circumvented by sign language and communication devices.

bibliography

Bibliography

Abilities Inc. of Florida. <u>Employment of the Physically Handicapped in a Competitive Industrial Environment</u>. Clearwater, Fla.: Author, 1966.

American Foundation for the Blind. <u>Aids and Appliances for the Blind and Visually Impaired</u>. New York: Author, 1976.

Ames, Thomas R. "Program Profiles: A Program for Transition to Independence." <u>Mental Retardation</u> 8 (April 1970): 49-51.

Banathy, Bela H. <u>Developing a Systems View of Education</u>. Belmont, Calif.: Lear Siegler/Fearon Publishers, 1973.

Bandura, Albert. <u>Principles of Behavior Modification</u>. New York: Holt, Rinehart, and Winston, 1965.

Baroff, George S. "The Vocational Potential of Mentally Retarded Persons." In <u>Adjustment to Work</u>, edited by J. G. Cull and R. E. Hardy. Springfield, Ill.: Charles C. Thomas, 1973.

Bean, Bonnie R., & Beard, John H. "Placement for Persons with Psychiatric Disability." <u>Rehabilitation Counseling Bulletin</u> 18 (June 1975): 253-258.

Bellamy, G. Thomas. "Habilitation of the Severely and Profoundly Retarded: A Review of Research on Work Productivity." In <u>Habilitation of the Severely and Profoundly Retarded: Reports from the Specialized Training Program</u>, edited by G. T. Bellamy. Eugene, Ore.: University of Oregon Center on Human Development, 1976.

Bellamy, G. Thomas; Peterson, Leslie; & Close, Daniel W. "Habilitation of the Severely and Profoundly Retarded: Illustrations of Competence." Clinical Research Paper No. 1, pp. 15-19. Eugene, Ore.: University of Oregon, Rehabilitation Research and Training Center in Mental Retardation, 1975.

Bentzen, B. L. "Transfer of Learning from School Setting to Life Style in a Habilitation Program for Multiply Handicapped Blind Persons." <u>New Outlook for the Blind</u> 67 (1973): 297-300.

Bitter, James A., & Bolanovitch, D. J. "The Habilitation Workshop in a Comprehensive Philosophy for Vocational Adjustment Training." <u>Rehabilitation Literature</u> 27 (November 1966): 330-332.

Brickey, Michael. "Normalization and Behavior Modification in the Workshop." <u>Journal of Rehabilitation</u>, November/December 1974: p. 15.

Brown, Lou; Van Deventer, Patricia; Perlmutter, Lucille; Jones, Stephen; & Sontag, Edward. "Effects of Consequences on Production Rates of Trainable Retarded and Severely Emotionally Disturbed Students in a Public School Workshop." <u>Education and Training of the Mentally Retarded</u> 7 (April 1972): 74-81.

Burleson, Georgia. "Modeling: An Effective Behavior Change Technique for Teaching Blind Persons." <u>New Outlook for the Blind</u> 67 (December 1973): p. 433.

Central Hospital. <u>Greentree School</u>. Lakeland, Ky.: Author, 1971.

Chacon, Carlos; Harper, P.; & Harvey, G. F. "Work Study in the Assessment of the Effects of Phenothiazines in Schizophrenia." <u>Comprehensive Psychiatry</u> 13 (November 1972): 549-554.

Chapanis, A. Man-Machine Engineering. Belmont, Calif.: Wadsworth Publishing Co., 1968.

Christensen, Nancy A.; Dubois, Phyllis A.; & Austin, Melanie. Selected Bibliography for Vocational Training and Placement of the Severely Handicapped. Palo Alto, Calif.: American Institutes for Research, 1975.

Clark, L. L. International Catalog: Aids and Appliances for Blind and Visually Impaired Persons. New York: American Foundation for the Blind, Inc., 1973.

Cohen, L. K. Communication Aids for the Brain-Damaged Adult. Minneapolis: Sister Kenny Institute, 1976.

Cortazzo, Arnold D., & Runnels, Eugene J. "One Approach to Rehabilitating the Retarded." Rehabilitation Literature 31 (December 1970): 354-360.

Craighead, W. Edward, & Mercatoris, Michael. "Mentally Retarded Residents as Paraprofessionals: A Review." American Journal of Mental Deficiency 78 (November 1973): 339-347.

Durand, John; Nelson, Howard F.; & O'Brien, Jeanne. "Handicapped Citizens Become First-Class Citizens at St. Paul's O.T.C." School Shop 32 (May 1973): 32-35.

Flanagan, John C.; Tiedeman, David V.; Willis, Mary B.; & McLaughlin, Donald H. The Career Data Book: Results from Project TALENT's Five-Year Follow-Up Study. Palo Alto, Calif.: American Institutes for Research, 1973.

Garris, A. G. Rehab Roundup Sacramento: California State Department of Vocational Rehabilitation, January 1974.

Garris, A. G. Rehab Roundup Sacramento: California State Department of Vocational Rehabilitation. May 1975.

Gold, Marc W. "Factors Affecting Production by the Retarded: Base Rate." Mental Retardation 11 (December 1973): 41-45.

Gold, Marc W. "Redundant Cue Removed in Skill Training for the Retarded." Education and Training of the Mentally Retarded 9 (February 1974): 5-8.

Gold, Marc W. "Stimulus Factors in Skill Training of Retarded Adolescents on a Complex Assembly Task: Acquisition, Transfer, and Retention." American Journal of Mental Deficiency 76 (March 1972): 517-526.

Gold, Marc W. "Vocational Training." In Mental Retardation and Developmental Disabilities. Volume VII, edited by Joseph Worties. New York: Brunner/Mazel Publishers, 1975.

Gold, Marc W., & Barclay, Craig R. "The Effects of Verbal Labels on the Acquisition and Retention of a Complex Assembly Task." Training School Bulletin 70 (May 1973): 38-42.

Greenleigh Associates, Inc. A Study to Develop a Model for Employment Services to the Handicapped. New York: Author, 1969.

Hildred, W. A Case Study of Technology Transfer: Rehabilitative Engineering at Rancho Los Amigos Hosptial. Denver: University of Denver, Denver Research Institute, 1973.

Hillam, B. "Shutterbugging Again." Rehabilitation Gazette 18, 1975.

Housman, R., & Gentile, F. "District Clerks Who Never Leave Home." School Management 16 (1972): 33-34.

Jackson, James L. "Extended Rehabilitation Services for the Mentally and Physically Handicapped." Rehabilitation Literature 32 (February 1971): 43-44.

Kidd, John W. "Potential for Employment of the Handicapped." In Contemporary Concepts in Vocational Education, edited by Gordon F. Law, pp. 81-86. Washington, D.C.: The American Vocational Association, 1971.

Knorr, K. H., & Hammond, N. C. "Data Processing--A Vocation for Severely Handicapped Persons." Journal of Rehabilitation 41 (6) 1975: 26-29.

Kruger, F. M. "The Role of Technology in Deaf-Blind Communication." Proceedings of 1976 Conference on Systems and Devices for the Disabled, 1976.

Lambert, R. H., et al. Modifying Regular Programs and Developing Curriculum Materials for the Vocational Education of the Handicapped. Progress Report. Madison: University of Wisconsin, Center for Studies in Vocational and Technical Education, 1975.

Laurence, Marilyn. "The Self-Reliance Institute: Filling the Gap in Work Experience." New Outlook for the Blind 67 (May 1973): 221-225.

Library of Congress, Division for the Blind and Physically Handicapped. Aids for Handicapped Readers. Author, 1972.

Lippman, Glenda K., & Porter, Grady C. How to Establish Competency Model Programs. Austin: Lippman/ Porter, 1976.

Luckey, Robert E., & Addison, Max R. "The Profoundly Retarded: A New Challenge for Public Education." Education and Training of the Mentally Retarded 9 (October 1974): 123-130.

Maley, Donald. Cluster Concept in Vocational Education. Chicago: American Technical Society, 1975.

Mann, R. "Kinesthetic Sensing for the EMG Controlled 'Boston Arm.'" IEEE Transactions of Man-Machine Systems 11 (1970): 110-115.

Mann, R. "Force and Position Proprioception." In The Control of Upper Extremity Prostheses, Orthoses, edited by Herberts et al. Springfield, Ill.: Charles C. Thomas, 1974.

National Association for Retarded Citizens. Guidelines for State and Local Vocational Rehabilitation and Employment Committees. Arlington, Texas: Author.

National Technical Institute for the Deaf. Job Accommodations for Deaf Employees. Rochester, New York: Author, n.d.

OPTACON Fund Quarterly Reports. Palo Alto, Calif.: OPTACON Fund.

Peterson, Richard O., & Jones, Edna M. Guide to Jobs for the Mentally Retarded. Washington, D.C.: American Institutes for Research, 1976.

President's Committee on Employment of the Handicapped. "Of Men and Machines." Performance 15, (1975): 9-11.

Rehabilitation Institute of Chicago. Access Chicago. Architects' and Designers' Handbook of Barrier-Free Design. Chicago: Author, n.d.

Rice, B. Douglas, & Milligan, Tim. "A Structured Approach to Independent Living Training for Young, Multiply Handicapped, Deaf Adults." Journal of Rehabilitation of the Deaf 6 (April 1973): 38-43.

Sloan, L. L. Recommended Aids for the Partially Sighted. New York: National Society for the Prevention of Blindness, 1971.

Smith, G. M. "The Telephone Company Message: 'Can Do!'" Rehabilitation Gazette 18 (1975): 42-43.

Staros, A., & Peizer, E. VA Prosthetics Center Research Report, n.p., 1975.

Stewart, Larry G. "Problems of Severely Handicapped Deaf: Implications for Educational Programs." American Annals of the Deaf 116 (June 1971): 362-368.

Szoke, Claire. "To Serve Those Who Are Handicapped: A Special Model Construct for Career Education." Illinois Career Education Journal 31 (Summer 1974): 2-5.

Trybus, Raymond J., & Lacks, Patricia B. "Modification of Vocational Behavior in a Community Agency for Mentally Retarded Adolescents." Rehabilitation Literature 33 (September 1972): 258-266.

University of California at Los Angeles, Division of Vocational Education. Cosmetology and the Physically Handicapped: Courses and Objectives. Los Angeles: Author, 1971.

U.S. Department of Labor. Dictionary of Occupational Titles, Third Edition. Washington, D.C.: U.S. Government Printing Office, 1965.

U.S. Department of Labor. Dictionary of Occupational Titles, Fourth Edition. Washington, D.C.: U.S. Government Printing Office, 1977.

U.S. Department of Labor, Manpower Administration. Interviewing Guides for Specific Disabilities. Washington, D.C.: Author, n.d.

U.S. Department of Transportation, Urban Mass Transportation Administration. A Directory of Vehicles and Related Systems Components for the Elderly and Handicapped. Washington, D.C.: U.S. Government Printing Office, 1975.

U.S. Office of Education, Bureau of Education for the Handicapped. Vocational Training and Placement of the Severely Handicapped. RFP #75-63. March 1975.

Yarbrough, Charles C. "Programming and Automated Recording in a Sheltered Workshop." Mental Retardation 10 (December 1972): 9-11.

Zamochnick, Alan D. "A Perspective on Deafness and Cerebral Palsy." Journal of Rehabilitation of the Deaf 7 (October 1973): 6-14.

Zimbardo, Philip, & Ebbesen, Ebbe B. Influencing Attitudes and Changing Behavior. Menlo Park, Calif.: Addison-Wesley Publishing Co., 1969.

AIDS AND DEVICES

Below is a list of aids and devices referred to in this handbook, along with addresses of the companies where they can be obtained. This is not intended to be a comprehensive list of available products.

1. Adjustable Wheelchair

> Motorette Corporation
> 6014 Reseda Blvd.
> Tarzana, CA 91356

2. Braille and "Talking" Calculators

> A.F.B. Calculator
> American Foundation for the Blind
> 15 West 16th St.
> New York, NY 10011
>
> Calcu-Tac Model T8B (braille output on
> paper tape--scientific calculator)
> Science for the Blind
> 221 Rock Hill Rd.
> Bala Cynwyd, PA 19004
>
> A.R.C. Model 9500 (talking)
> Master Specialties Company
> 647 Babcock Rd.
> Costa Mesa, CA 92627
>
> Speech Plus Talking Calculator
> Telesensory Systems, Inc.
> 1889 Page Mill Rd.
> Palo Alto, CA 94304

3. E-Z Reacher

> Physical Aids Manufacturing Co.
> 4848 Ronson Ct.
> San Diego, CA 92111

4. OPTACON

> Telesensory Systems, Inc.
> 1889 Page Mill Rd.
> Palo Alto, CA 94304

5. Braille Computer

> Protestant Guild for the Blind
> 465 Belmont St.
> Watertown, MA 02172

6. Sensory Aids Catalog (forthcoming)

> Sensory Aids Foundation
> 399 Sherman Ave.
> Palo Alto, CA 94306

7. Stereotoner

> Mauch Laboratories, Inc.
> 3035 Dryden Rd.
> Dayton, OH 45439

8. Telephone Add-Ons

> Contact any telephone company business office.
> The Bell Telephone System's booklet, "Services
> for Special Needs," which describes telephone
> modifications, is available upon request.

9. Braille Computer Terminal

> Triformation Systems, Inc.
> P.O. Box 2433
> Stuart, FL 33494

10. Prostheses

> Veteran's Administration
> Research Center for Prosthetics
> 252 Seventh Ave.
> New York, NY 10001

ASSOCIATIONS AND COMMITTEES

1. American Mutual Insurance Alliance
    20 North Wacker Dr.
    Chicago, IL 60606

2. Chamber of Commerce of the U.S.
    1615 H St. N.W.
    Washington, D.C. 20006

3. National Association of Manufacturers
    Employee Relations Division
    277 Park Ave.
    New York, NY 10805

4. President's Committee on Employment of the Handicapped
    Washington, D.C. 20210

PROGRAMS

1. Children's Hospital at Stanford
    Rehabilitation Engineering Center
    Stanford, CA 94305

2. Regional Transportation District
    Special Needs Program
    1325 So. Colorado Blvd.
    Denver, CO 80222

3. Trace Research and Development Center for the Severely Communicatively Impaired
    University of Wisconsin
    922 E.R.B.
    1500 Johnson Dr.
    Madison, WI 53706

appendix

THE DICTIONARY OF OCCUPATIONAL TITLES (DOT)

The <u>Dictionary</u> <u>of</u> <u>Occupational</u> <u>Titles</u> (DOT) is a standard
source of occupational information put out by the U.S. Depart-
ment of Labor. The fourth edition, published in 1977, is
the most complete listing of American job opportunities
currently available. The following pages, from the DOT,
describe the coding system in detail.

The *Dictionary of Occupational Titles* is an outgrowth of the needs of the public employment service system for a comprehensive body of standardized occupational information for purposes of job placement, employment counseling
and occupational and career guidance, and for labor market information services. In order to implement effectively its primary assignment of matching jobs
and workers, the public employment service system requires a uniform occupational language for use in all of its offices. This is needed to compare and
match the specifications of employer job openings and the qualifications of
applicants who are seeking jobs through its facilities.

The need for this type of occupational descriptive information was recognized
in the mid-1930's, within a few years after the passage of the Wagner-Peyser
Act, establishing a Federal-State employment service system. An occupational
research program was initiated, as one facet of public employment service operations, using analysts located in several field stations scattered throughout
the country to collect the information required. Based on these data, the first
edition of the *Dictionary of Occupational Titles* was published in 1939.

That edition contained a total of almost 17,500 concise definitions presented
alphabetically, by title, with a coding arrangement for occupational classification. Blocks of jobs were assigned 5- or 6-digit codes which placed them in
one of 550 occupational groups and indicated if the jobs were skilled, semi-
skilled or unskilled.

Comprehensive updates of the *Dictionary* were issued in 1949, with the release
of the second edition of the DOT, and in 1965 when the third edition was published. The second edition reflected, to some extent, the impact of World War
II on jobs in the U.S. economy. To fill the widening gap between occupational
information needed and that available, several supplements to the 1939 edition
were issued throughout the war period. By 1945, with the release of the third
and final supplement to the first edition, a total of more than 6,100 new occupational definitions had been published.

The revised second edition, issued in March 1949, combined material in the
first edition with its supplements. It was also expanded to include new occupations in the plastics, paper and pulp, and radio manufacturing industries.

Material used in conjunction with the second edition included information,
which was first released in a World War II supplement, relating to occupational
classification of entry applicants with no previous work experience. This was
done through a secondary occupational coding system—the Entry Occupational
Classification Structure. Under that coding structure, jobs were grouped in
terms of factors that could indicate the applicant's readiness and preference
for specific jobs.

The third edition eliminated the previous Departmental designation of certain
jobs as being "skilled, semi-skilled or unskilled," and substituted a classifica-

tion system based both on the nature of the work performed and the demands of such work activities upon the workers. These indicators of work requirements included eight separate classification components: training time, aptitudes, interests, temperaments, physical demands, working conditions, work performed, and industry.

The 1977 edition is the result of continued research on the changing occupational structure of the American economy, conducted by the U.S. Employment Service and job analysts in affiliated State Employment Service Occupational Analysis Field Centers throughout the country. Users of the third edition should have no difficulty in making the transition to this volume. None of the changes introduce content or concepts unfamiliar to users of the previous edition. This edition retains the breakdown of occupations into categories, divisions, and groups, although the occupational codes for some divisions and groups have been revised. Worker functions ratings, first introduced in the third edition, have been retained as well. However, for many occupational titles, the three middle digits of the 9-digit occupational code have been changed to reflect actual worker functions ratings. The changes in the new edition are designed to establish a broader occupational base for such purposes as classifying job applications and job orders, making referrals, assessing worker transferability into related jobs, or relocating workers displaced by technological change.[1]

The material included in the third edition of the DOT was compiled mostly in the early 1960's or even earlier. The rapid changes in industrial technology since that time have been accompanied by significant modifications in the characteristics and job requirements of many occupations. To keep abreast of these developments, analysts on State Occupational Analysis Field Center staffs, as part of the Employment Service occupational analysis program, make on-site job analyses of the spectrum of jobs in various industries to verify or revise the definitions of occupations listed in the DOT. These job analyses are designed to insure that the job definitions listed in the DOT are not based on obsolescent industrial practices which are no longer commonly used in the production of goods and services in the United States.

The fourth edition is based on more than 75,000 such on-site analyses conducted from 1965 to the early- and mid-1970's, and on extensive contacts with professional and trade associations. These activities were designed to reverify and reevaluate the job content and definitions of the occupations listed in the DOT and to identify new occupations. As a result of this program, over 2,100 new occupational definitions were added and some 3,500 deleted as compared with the third edition. Many thousand other descriptions were substantially modified or combined with closely related definitions to eliminate overlap and duplication, and to reflect the consolidation and restructuring of some occupations. The fourth edition contains approximately 20,000 jobs, about 1,800 less than in the third edition.

As this edition goes to press, a number of State employment service offices are computerized; most are not. Over the next half dozen years, the Employment Service will operate partly in a manual, and partly in a computerized mode. Changes in the new edition of the *Dictionary* were minimized to take account of this transition period. In future editions, after computerization is completed, refinements and innovations will be introduced which should help integrate the basic concepts in the DOT with the supplementary occupational classifica-

---

[1]See p. xxiv for a more detailed comparison of the third and fourth editions.

tion tools used in computerized job matching, such as the *Handbook of Occupational Keywords.*

The occupational codes and titles used in this edition should also permit a more effective interchange of occupational data among government agencies. Work was underway in 1977 to relate the classification system in the *Dictionary* to other government occupational language systems such as those of the Bureau of the Census, the Bureau of Labor Statistics, the U.S. Office of Education, and the Office of Management and Budget, Standard Occupational Classification (SOC) program. A joint project of the Labor and Defense Departments already has related occupational titles in the *Dictionary* to those in the military service in order to smooth the transition of persons between military and civilian life. A supplement to the *Dictionary,* in preparation as this edition went to press, is designed for use by the Social Security Administration as a guide to possible new careers for disabled workers and to determine benefit eligibility.

In using the *Dictionary,* one should note that the U.S. Employment Service has no responsibility for establishing appropriate wage levels for workers in the United States, or setting jurisdictional matters in relation to different occupations. In preparing job definitions, no data were collected concerning these and related matters. Therefore, the occupational information in this edition cannot be regarded as determining standards for any aspect of the employer-employee relationship.

Parts of the Occupational Definition

Work is organized in a variety of ways. As a result of technological, economic and sociological influences, nearly every job in the economy is performed slightly differently from any other job. Every job is also similar to a number of other jobs.

In order to look at the millions of jobs in the U.S. economy in an organized way, the DOT groups jobs into "occupations" based on their similarities and defines the structure and content of all listed occupations. Occupational definitions are the result of comprehensive studies of how similar jobs are performed in establishments all over the nation and are composites of data collected from diverse sources. The term "occupation," as used in the DOT, refers to this collective description of a number of individual jobs performed, with minor variations, in many establishments.

There are six basic parts to an occupational definition. They present data about a job in a systematic fashion. The parts are listed below in the order in which they appear in every definition:

(1) The Occupational Code Number
(2) The Occupational Title
(3) The Industry Designation
(4) Alternate Titles (if any)
(5) The Body of the Definition
    (a) Lead statement
    (b) Task element statements
    (c) "May" items
(6) Undefined Related Titles (if any)

A typical DOT definition (with each of the six parts labeled) is analyzed on the following page:

PARTS OF A DOT DEFINITION

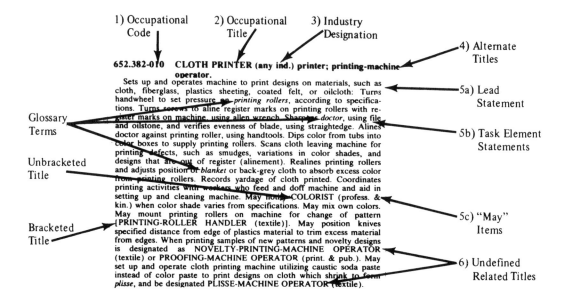

1) Occupational Code   2) Occupational Title   3) Industry Designation

4) Alternate Titles

652.382-010 CLOTH PRINTER (any ind.) printer; printing-machine operator.

Sets up and operates machine to print designs on materials, such as cloth, fiberglass, plastics sheeting, coated felt, or oilcloth: Turns handwheel to set pressure on *printing rollers*, according to specifications. Turns screws to aline register marks on printing rollers with register marks on machine, using allen wrench. Sharpens *doctor*, using file and oilstone, and verifies evenness of blade, using straightedge. Alines doctor against printing roller, using handtools. Dips color from tubs into color boxes to supply printing rollers. Scans cloth leaving machine for printing defects, such as smudges, variations in color shades, and designs that are out of register (alinement). Realines printing rollers and adjusts position of *blanket* or back-grey cloth to absorb excess color from printing rollers. Records yardage of cloth printed. Coordinates printing activities with workers who feed and doff machine and aid in setting up and cleaning machine. May notify COLORIST (profess. & kin.) when color shade varies from specifications. May mix own colors. May mount printing rollers on machine for change of pattern [PRINTING-ROLLER HANDLER (textile)]. May position knives specified distance from edge of plastics material to trim excess material from edges. When printing samples of new patterns and novelty designs is designated as NOVELTY-PRINTING-MACHINE OPERATOR (textile) or PROOFING-MACHINE OPERATOR (print. & pub.). May set up and operate cloth printing machine utilizing caustic soda paste instead of color paste to print designs on cloth which shrink to form *plisse*, and be designated PLISSE-MACHINE OPERATOR (textile).

Glossary Terms

Unbracketed Title

Bracketed Title

5a) Lead Statement

5b) Task Element Statements

5c) "May" Items

6) Undefined Related Titles

(1) The Occupational Code Number

The first item in an occupational definition is the 9-digit occupational code (in the example, 652.382-010). In the DOT occupational classification system, each set of three digits in the 9-digit code number has a specific purpose or meaning. Together, they provide a unique identification code for a particular occupation which differentiates it from all others.

The *first three digits* identify a particular occupational group. All occupations are clustered into one of nine broad "categories" (first digit), such as professional, technical and managerial, or clerical and sales occupations. These categories break up into 82 occupationally specific "divisions" (first two digits), such as occupations in architecture and engineering within the professional category, or stenography, typing, filing and related occupations in the clerical and sales category. Divisions, in turn, separate into small, homogeneous "groups" (first three digits)—559 such groups are identified in the DOT. The nine primary occupational categories are listed below:

0/1   Professional, Technical, and Managerial Occupations

2   Clerical and Sales Occupations

3 Service Occupations
4 Agricultural, Fishery, Forestry, and Related Occupations
5 Processing Occupations
6 Machine Trades Occupations
7 Bench Work Occupations
8 Structural Work Occupations
9 Miscellaneous Occupations

In the example, the first digit (6) indicates that this particular occupation is found in the category, "Machine Trades Occupations."[2]

The second digit refers to a division within the category. The divisions within the "Machines Trades Occupations" category are as follows:

60 Metal Machining Occupations
61 Metalworking Occupations, n.e.c.
62/63 Mechanics and Machinery Repairers
64 Paperworking Occupations
65 Printing Occupations
66 Wood Machining Occupations
67 Occupations in Machining Stone, Clay, Glass and Related Materials
68 Textile Occupations
69 Machine Trades Occupations, n.e.c.[3]

In the example, the second digit (5) thus locates the occupation in the "Printing Occupations" division.

The third digit defines the occupational group within the division. The groups within the "Printing Occupations" division are as follows:

650 Typesetters and Composers
651 Printing Press Occupations
652 Printing Machine Occupations
653 Bookbinding-Machine Operators and Related Occupations
654 Typecasters and Related Occupations
659 Printing Occupations, n.e.c.

The third digit in the example (2) locates the occupation in the "Printing Machine Occupations" group.

The *middle three digits* of the DOT occupational code are the worker functions ratings of the tasks performed in the occupation. Every job requires a worker to function to some degree in relation to data, people, and things. A separate digit expresses the worker's relationship to each of these three groups:

---

[2]For a listing of all occupational categories, divisions, and groups see p. xxxiv.

[3]Some divisions or groups end in the designation "n.e.c." (not elsewhere classified). This indicates that the occupations do not logically fit into more precisely defined divisions or groups, or that they could fit into two or more of them equally well.

DATA (4th Digit)	PEOPLE (5th Digit)	THINGS (6th Digit)
0 Synthesizing	0 Mentoring	0 Setting Up
1 Coordinating	1 Negotiating	1 Precision Working
2 Analyzing	2 Instructing	2 Operating-Controlling
3 Compiling	3 Supervising	3 Driving-Operating
4 Computing	4 Diverting	4 Manipulating
5 Copying	5 Persuading	5 Tending
6 Comparing	6 Speaking-Signalling	6 Feeding-Offbearing
	7 Serving	7 Handling
	8 Taking Instructions-Helping	

Worker functions involving more complex responsibility and judgment are assigned lower numbers in these three lists while functions which are less complicated have higher numbers. For example, "synthesizing" and "coordinating" data are more complex tasks than "copying" data; "instructing" people involves a broader responsibility than "taking instructions-helping"; and "operating" things is a more complicated task than "handling" things.

The worker functions code in the example (382) relates to the middle three digits of the DOT occupational code and has a different meaning and no necessary connection with group code 652 (first three digits).

The worker functions [4] code (382) may relate to any occupational group. It signifies that the worker is "compiling" in relation to data (3); "taking instructions-helping" in relation to people (8); and "operating-controlling" in relation to things (2). The worker functions code indicates the broadest level of responsibility or judgment required in relation to data, people, or things. It is assumed that, if the job requires it, the worker can generally perform any higher numbered function listed in each of the three categories.

The *last three digits* of the occupational code number indicate the alphabetical order of titles within 6-digit code groups. They serve to differentiate a particular occupation from all others. A number of occupations may have the same first six digits, but no two can have the same nine digits. If a 6-digit code is applicable to only one occupational title, the final three digits assigned are always 010 (as in the example). If there is more than one occupation with the same first six digits, the final three digits are usually assigned in alphabetical order of titles in multiples of four (010, 014, 018, 022, etc.). If another printing machine occupation had the same six digits as CLOTH PRINTER (any ind.), and began with the letter "D," it would be assigned the occupational code 652.382-014.

The full nine digits thus provide each occupation with a unique code suitable for computerized operations.

(2) The Occupational Title

Immediately following the occupational code in every definition is the occupational base title. The base title is always in upper-case boldface letters. It is the most common type of title found in the DOT, and is the title by which the occupation is known in the majority of establishments in which it was found. In the example, CLOTH PRINTER (any ind.) is a base title.

---

[4]See appendix for more detailed discussion of worker functions codes.

Some titles are classified as *master titles*. These titles are designed to eliminate unnecessary repetition of tasks common to a large number of occupations. Master titles define the common job tasks having a wide variety of job variables and a wide variety of titles. An example is the title "SUPERVISOR (any ind.)." Each individual supervisory occupation has its own separate definition in the DOT describing its unique duties, but at the end of the definition the reader is referred back to the master definition (in this case, by a sentence reading "Performs other duties as described under SUPERVISOR (any ind.)." By referring to this master definition, the user will learn about the typical supervisory duties which any individual supervisor also performs.

Another type of DOT title is a *term title*. These include occupations with the same title but few common duties. An example of a term definition is:

> CONSULTING ENGINEER (profess. & kin.): A term applied to workers who consult with and advise clients on specialized engineering matters in a particular field of endeavor, such as chemical engineering, civil engineering, or mechanical engineering.

Since neither master nor term definitions are occupations, they are not coded in the occupational group arrangement but are found in separate sections of the DOT (see Contents).

There are other major types of titles used in the DOT, including *alternate titles* and *undefined related titles*. These are discussed later in this subsection of the Introduction.

(3) Industry Designation

The industry designation is in parentheses immediately following the occupational base title. It often differentiates between two or more occupations with identical titles but different duties. Because of this, it is an integral and inseparable part of any occupational title. An industry designation often tells one or more things about an occupation such as:

-location of the occupation (hotel & rest.; mach. shop)
-types of duties associated with the occupation (clean., dye. & press.; education)
-products manufactured (textile; optical goods)
-processes used (electroplating; petrol. refin.)
-raw materials used (nonfer. metal alloys; stonework)

While a definition usually receives the designation of the industry or industries in which it occurs, certain occupations occur in a large number of industries. When this happens, the industry is assigned a cross-industry designation. For example, clerical occupations are found in almost every industry. To show the broad, cross-industry nature of clerical occupations, "clerical" is an industry designation in itself. Among other cross-industry designations are: "profess. & kin.," "mach. shop," and "woodworking."

Occupations which occur in a number of industries, but are not found so widely as to warrant their own industry designation, are given the designation of "any industry." The job title in the example is given this designation. It should always be given as CLOTH PRINTER (any ind.).[5]

---

[5]In compiling information for the DOT, analysts were not able to study each occupation in all industries where it occurs. The industry designation, therefore, shows in what industries the occupation was studied but does not mean that it may not be found in others. Therefore, industry designations are to be regarded as indicative of industrial location, but not necessarily restrictive.

(4) Alternate Titles

An alternate title is a synonym for the base title. It is not as commonly used as the base title. Alternate titles are shown in lower-case boldface letters immediately after the base title and its industrial designation. In our example, two alternate titles are given: "printer" and "printing-machine operator." Alternate titles may not be used by public employment service offices in assigning occupational classifications. Alternate titles are cross-referenced to their base titles in the Alphabetical Index of Occupational Titles (p. 965). A particular occupation may have a large number of alternate titles or none at all. Alternate titles carry the code numbers and industry designations of the base title.

(5) The Body of the Definition

The body of the definition usually consists of two or three main parts: a lead statement, a number of task element statements, and a third part known as a "may" item.

(a) The Lead Statement

The first sentence following the industry designation and alternate titles (if any) is the lead statement. It is followed by a colon (:). The lead statement summarizes the entire occupation. It offers essential information such as:

-worker actions
-the objective or purpose of the worker actions
-machines, tools, equipment, or work aids used by the worker
-materials used, products made, subject matter dealt with, or services rendered
-instructions followed or judgments made

In the example, the sentence "Sets up and operates machine to print designs on materials such as cloth, fiberglass, plastics sheeting, coated felt, or oilcloth:" is the lead statement. From it, the user can obtain an overview of the occupation.

(b) Task Element Statements

Task element statements indicate the specific tasks the worker performs to accomplish the overall job purpose described in the lead statement. The sentences in the example beginning with "Turns handwheel. . .", "Turns screws . . .", "Sharpens doctor . . .", "Alines doctor . . .",[6] "Dips color . . .", etc. are all task element statements. They indicate how the worker actually carries out his or her duties.

(c) "May" Items

Many definitions contain one or more sentences beginning with the word "May." They describe duties required of workers in this occupation in some establishments but not in others. The word "May" does *not* indicate that a worker will sometimes perform this task but rather that some workers in different establishments generally perform one of

---

[6]The spelling of certain words in the DOT (such as "aline" in the example) conform to *U.S. Government Printing Office Style Manual* regulations. See Glossary for explanation of specialized meaning of the word "doctor" in this context.

the varied tasks listed. In the example, the three sentences beginning "May notify . . .", "May mount . . .", "May position . . .", are "May" items.[7]

The definition also contains a number of additional information elements designed to assist the user. Among these elements are:

Italicized words: Any words in a definition shown in italics are defined in the "Glossary" (p. 947). They are technical terms or special uses of terms not ordinarily found in a standard dictionary (in the example, the words "printing rollers," "doctor," and "blanket" are italicized. Their precise meaning can be found in the "Glossary").

Bracketed titles: A bracketed title indicates that the worker in the base title occupation performs some duties of the bracketed occupation as a part of his regular duties. In the example, the CLOTH PRINTER (any ind.) "May mount printing rollers . . . ." Since this task is usually performed by a PRINTER-ROLLER HANDLER (textile), this occupation is bracketed. To learn more about this particular aspect of the occupation, the user can look up the bracketed occupational title.

Unbracketed titles: Unbracketed titles are used for occupations whose workers have a frequent working relationship with workers in the occupation being defined. In the example, the CLOTH PRINT-ER (any ind.) may have a close working relationship with a COLOR-IST (profess. & kin.). This unbracketed title is therefore included in the definition.

Roman numerals: Several somewhat different occupations with the same job title may be found in the same industry. In this event, a Roman numeral follows each title and industry designation. For example, there are three titles in the DOT listed as ASSEMBLER (firearms). In order to distinguish between them, a Roman numeral is assigned to each one (ASSEMBLER (firearms) I, ASSEMBLER (firearms) II, etc.). There is no necessary connection in the sequence of these numbers with the level of complexity of these occupations or the frequency with which they occur in the U.S. economy.

Statement of significant variables: Another element found in some definitions is a statement of significant variables. It appears near the end of a definition and shows the possible variations in jobs that a particular definition can cover. This eliminates the need to include a large number of almost identical definitions in the DOT. The statement begins with "Important variations include. . . ." There is no statement of significant variables in the definition of CLOTH PRINT-ER (any ind.).

(6) Undefined Related Titles

Undefined related titles, if applicable, appear at the end of the occupational definition, in all capital letters, preceded by the phrase, "May be designated according to. . ." (or a similar phase). In the example, three undefined related titles, are given: NOVELTY-PRINTING-MACHINE-OPERATOR (textile), PROOFING-MACHINE OPERATOR (print. & pub.), and

---

[7]Do not confuse "May" items with the "May be designated. . ." sentence which introduced undefined related titles.

PLISSE-MACHINE OPERATOR (textile). This type of title is for an occupation that is really a variation or specialization of the base occupation. It resembles the base enough to accompany it, but differs from it enough to require an explanatory phrase and its own unique title. An undefined related title takes the same code as its base title. Undefined related titles found in occupational definitions are also listed in the Alphabetical Index of Occupational Titles with their industry designation and the 9-digit codes of their base titles. In addition, they appear in the list of Occupational Titles Arranged by Industry Designation in alphabetical order with 9-digit base title codes, within the appropriate industry.

APPENDIX

Explanation of Data, People and Things

Much of the information in this publication is based on the premise that every job requires a worker to function in some degree to Data, People and Things. These relationships are identified and explained below. They appear in the form of three listings arranged in each instance from the relatively simple to the complex in such a manner that each successive relationship includes those that are simpler and excludes the more complex.[1] The identifications attached to these relationships are referred to as worker functions, and provide standard terminology for use in summarizing exactly what a worker does on the job.

A job's relationship to Data, People and Things can be expressed in terms of the lowest numbered function in each sequence. These functions taken together indicate the total level of complexity at which the worker performs. The fourth, fifth and sixth digits of the occupational code numbers reflect relationships to Data, People and Things, respectively.[2] These digits express a job's relationship to Data, People and Things by identifying the highest appropriate function in each listing as reflected by the following table:

DATA (4th digit)	PEOPLE (5th digit)	THINGS (6th digit)
0 Synthesizing	0 Mentoring	0 Setting-Up
1 Coordinating	1 Negotiating	1 Precision Working
2 Analyzing	2 Instructing	2 Operating-Controlling
3 Compiling	3 Supervising	3 Driving-Operating
4 Computing	4 Diverting	4 Manipulating
5 Copying	5 Persuading	5 Tending
6 Comparing	6 Speaking-Signaling	6 Feeding - Offbearing
	7 Serving	7 Handling
	8 Taking Instructions - Helping	

Definitions of Worker Functions

DATA: Information, knowledge, and conceptions, related to data, people, or things, obtained by observation, investigation, interpretation, visualization, and mental creation. Data are intangible and include numbers, words, symbols, ideas, concepts, and oral verbalization.

0 Synthesizing: Integrating analyses of data to discover facts and/or develop knowledge concepts or interpretations.

1 Coordinating: Determining time, place, and sequence of operations or action to be taken on the basis of analysis of data; executing determination and/or reporting on events.

2 Analyzing: Examining and evaluating data. Presenting alternative actions in relation to the evaluation is frequently involved.

---

[1]As each of the relationships to People represents a wide range of complexity, resulting in considerable overlap among occupations, their arrangement is somewhat arbitrary and can be considered a hierarchy only in the most general sense.

[2]Only those relationships which are occupationally significant in terms of the requirements of the job are reflected in the code numbers. The incidental relationships which every worker has to Data, People, and Things, but which do not seriously affect successful performance of the essential duties of the job, are not reflected.

3. Compiling: Gathering, collating, or classifying information about data, people, or things. Reporting and/or carrying out a prescribed action in relation to the information is frequently involved.

4 Computing: Performing arithmetic operations and reporting on and/or carrying out a prescribed action in relation to them. Does not include counting.

5 Copying: Transcribing, entering, or posting data.

6 Comparing: Judging the readily observable functional, structural, or compositional characteristics (whether similar to or divergent from obvious standards) of data, people, or things.

PEOPLE: Human beings; also animals dealt with on an individual basis as if they were human.

0 Mentoring: Dealing with individuals in terms of their total personality in order to advise, counsel, and/or guide them with regard to problems that may be resolved by legal, scientific, clinical, spiritual, and/or other professional principles.

1 Negotiating: Exchanging ideas, information, and opinions with others to formulate policies and programs and/or arrive jointly at decisions, conclusions, or solutions.

2 Instructing: Teaching subject matter to others, or training others (including animals) through explanation, demonstration, and supervised practice; or making recommendations on the basis of technical disciplines.

3. Supervising: Determining or interpreting work procedures for a group of workers, assigning specific duties to them, maintaining harmonious relations among them, and promoting efficiency. A variety of responsibilities is involved in this function.

4 Diverting: Amusing others. (Usually accomplished through the medium of stage, screen, television, or radio.)

5 Persuading: Influencing others in favor of a product, service, or point of view.

6 Speaking-Signaling: Talking with and/or signaling people to convey or exchange information. Includes giving assignments and/or directions to helpers or assistants.

7 Serving: Attending to the needs or requests of people or animals or the expressed or implicit wishes of people. Immediate response is involved.

8 Taking Instructions-Helping: Helping applies to "non-learning" helpers. No variety of responsibility is involved in this function.

THINGS: Inanimate objects as distinguished from human beings, substances or materials; machines, tools, equipment and products. A thing is tangible and has shape, form, and other physical characteristics.

0 Setting up: Adjusting machines or equipment by replacing or altering tools, jigs, fixtures, and attachments to prepare them to perform their functions,

change their performance, or restore their proper functioning if they break down. Workers who set up one or a number of machines for other workers or who set up and personally operate a variety of machines are included here.

1 Precision Working: Using body members and/or tools or work aids to work, move, guide, or place objects or materials in situations where ultimate responsibility for the attainment of standards occurs and selection of appropriate tools, objects, or materials, and the adjustment of the tool to the task require exercise of considerable judgment.

2 Operating-Controlling: Starting, stopping, controlling, and adjusting the progress of machines or equipment. Operating machines involves setting up and adjusting the machine or material(s) as the work progresses. Controlling involves observing gages, dials, etc., and turning valves and other devices to regulate factors such as temperature, pressure, flow of liquids, speed of pumps, and reactions of materials.

3 Driving-Operating: Starting, stopping, and controlling the actions of machines or equipment for which a course must be steered, or which must be guided, in order to fabricate, process, and/or move things or people. Involves such activities as observing gages and dials; estimating distances and determining speed and direction of other objects; turning cranks and wheels; pushing or pulling gear lifts or levers. Includes such machines as cranes, conveyor systems, tractors, furnace charging machines, paving machines and hoisting machines. Excludes manually powered machines, such as hand-trucks and dollies, and power assisted machines, such as electric wheelbarrows and handtrucks.

4 Manipulating: Using body members, tools, or special devices to work, move, guide, or place objects or materials. Involves some latitude for judgment with regard to precision attained and selecting appropriate tool, object, or material, although this is readily manifest.

5 Tending: Starting, stopping, and observing the functioning of machines and equipment. Involves adjusting materials or controls of the machine, such as changing guides, adjusting timers and temperature gages. turning valves to allow flow of materials, and flipping switches in response to lights. Little judgment is involved in making these adjustments.

6 Feeding-Offbearing: Inserting, throwing, dumping, or placing materials in or removing them from machines or equipment which are automatic or tended or operated by other workers.

7 Handling: Using body members, handtools, and/or special devices to work, move or carry objects or materials. Involves little or no latitude for judgment with regard to attainment of standards or in selecting appropriate tool, object, or material.

DATE DUE